The Power of
Infinite Love & Gratitude

AN EVOLUTIONARY JOURNEY TO AWAKENING YOUR SPIRIT

The Power of
Infinite Love & Gratitude

AN EVOLUTIONARY JOURNEY TO AWAKENING YOUR SPIRIT

Dr. Darren R. Weissman

Infinite Love Press
Riverwoods, Illinois

Publisher's Notes:

All matters regarding your health require medical supervision. The ideas, procedures and suggestions contained in this book are not intended as a substitute for consulting with your physician. The author and the publisher are not engaged in rendering professional advice or services to the individual reader and neither are responsible for your specific health needs that may require medical attention and/or supervision. Neither the author nor the publisher shall be liable or responsible for any loss or damage allegedly arising from any information or suggestion in this book.

All stories in this book are true; however, all patient names are fictitious to maintain patient confidentiality.

Reprinted with permission

Cover art and poem, "The Awakening," by Ranel Gretebeck. Reprinted with permission of the artist/author.

"I Love You" in sign language art by Rick Outten. Reprinted with permission of the artist.

"Our deepest fear . . . automatically liberates others." From *A Return to Love* by Marianne Williamson, Copyright © 1992, reprinted by permission of HarperCollins Publishers Inc. Portions reprinted from *A Course In Miracles*. Copyright © 1975 by Foundation for Inner Peace, Inc. All chapter openings are from *A Course in Miracles*.

Excerpts and photographs from *Messages from Water* by Dr. Masaru Emoto, Copyright © 1999 by Hado Kyoikusha, reprinted by permission of the author.

Excerpts from *Psycho-Cybernetics* by Maxwell Maltz, M.D., F.I.C.S., Copyright © 1960, reprinted by permission of the Psycho-Cybernetics Foundation, Inc., www.psycho-cybernetics.com.

"Autobiography in Five Chapters," Copyright © 1993 by Portia Nelson, from the book, *There's A Hole in My Sidewalk*. Reprinted by permission of Beyond Words Publishing, Inc., Hillsboro, Oregon, USA.

Excerpts from *Why People Don't Heal and How They Can* by Dr. Caroline Myss, published by Three Rivers Press, a division of Crown Publishers, Inc., Random House, Inc., Copyright © 1997, reprinted by permission of the publisher.

Excerpts from *Your Body's Many Cries for Water* by Fereydoon Batmanghelidj, M.D, Copyright © 1997, reprinted by permission of the author.

Excerpts from *Your Body Speaks Your Mind; How Your Thoughts and Emotions Affect Your Health* by Debbie Shapiro, Copyright © 1996, reprinted by permission of the author.

The poem, "Treasure of Love," by Kristin Dawson, Copyright © 2002, reprinted by permission of the author.

Published by Infinite Love Press, Riverwoods, Illinois

Printed in the United States of America

Library of Congress Cataloging-in-Publication Data

Weissman, Darren R.
  The Power of Infinite Love & Gratitude
  Darren R. Weissman – 1st Ed.
  Includes bibliographical references
ISBN 0-9744700-0-7

First Edition

For my beautiful wife, Sarit,
and our daughter, Joya Ruth,
with Infinite Love & Gratitude

With deepest appreciation to:

The Barefoot Doctors of China
Edgar Cayce
Dr. George Goodheart
Dr. Victor Frank
Dr. Scott Walker
Dr. Jon Sunderlage
Dr. Ralph Alan Dale
Dr. Steve Ciolino
Lord Pandit Professor Dr. Sir Anton Jayasuriya
Bob Warwick
Dr. Bruce Lipton
Richard Bandler
John Grinder
Dr. Masaru Emoto
Dr. Francine Shapiro
Dr. Candice Pert
Dr. Caroline Myss

Without your courage, determination and commitment to explore the frontiers and expand the boundaries of holistic medicine, my work would not be possible.

The LifeLine Technique follows in the footsteps of the Masters, carving out a new road.

To extend and expand the path that the mentor has graciously opened is the disciple's mission.

Table of Contents

Table of Contents

Author's Foreword

It has been said, "at the point of complete darkness is the beginning of light." My journey, like so many, began as a "wounded healer." As a child I have memories of feeling hopeless, suffering with multiple food and environmental allergies, asthma and chronic ear infections. I received weekly allergy shots and used bronchial inhalers both preventatively as well as during moments of labored breathing. At the age of seven, I had my tonsils and adenoids removed and had tubes surgically implanted in my ears to "cure" chronic infections that multiple rounds of antibiotics had not helped. There were many occasions that I was rushed to the emergency room for life-threatening asthma attacks. My diet consisted of fast food, Wonder Bread, Cocoa Puffs, pasta, soda and many other foods that had a high sugar content.

My paradigm of health was shaped by my experiences and the beliefs and values of the society in which I was raised. My parents, along with most people, used the medical model of taking a pill for every symptom as their primary frame of reference. Consequently, before I was old enough to learn the multiplication tables, I knew the names of more than a dozen medications that I was taking for symptoms with which I suffered all year long. My pediatrician said I would be an asthmatic for the rest of my life.

Fortunately, my parents raised me with the belief that every challenge is an opportunity. I am grateful for the health challenges I experienced during my childhood. It is because of those challenges that I chose to step beyond the boundaries of what I knew to discover the answers that would truly enable my body and mind to heal.

My journey to heal myself has taken me around the world to Sri Lanka, China, Belgium and throughout the United States. I have been on a mission to study with the most renowned healers and doctors of our time. I have been a sponge for information—reading books, watching videos, attending seminars and learning from life's experiences. Everything I learned became a stepping stone for my own healing from asthma, allergies, an inguinal hernia, a left testicular mass, bulging discs, addiction, a ruptured achilles tendon, learning disabilities, parasites, vitiligo and a slew of many other symptoms and challenges. Using natural healing modalities, I faced and conquered each of these challenges. As a consequence, I developed a new and deeper understanding of the nature of symptoms. The culmination of my journey has led me to awaken to a system of healing, the philosophy of which is the basis of this book.

My journey to healing has helped me recognize that there is always hope in life. You just need to have determination, trust your intuition and open your heart to find it. For me, hope began with a telephone call.

During the second semester of my sophomore year at the University of Kansas, where I was taking pre-med courses to prepare for medical school, my brother Howie was involved in a serious car accident. He initially was treated with muscle relaxants and anti-inflammatory drugs. But Howie soon discovered that the treatments were unsuccessful and there were other, unwanted side effects. One month after the accident, he called to share an amazing experience—his body had completely recovered as the result of treatments by a chiropractic physician. I will always remember his exact words: "Darren, you have got to check out chiropractic! I think this is the profession for you."

I had never been to a chiropractor and had no idea what they did. I looked in the telephone directory and began to call local chiropractors in Lawrence, Kansas. Twenty calls later, I reached Dr. James Dray. He told me that he was in the process of relocating his office. If I helped him with the packing and moving, he said he would teach me about chiropractic. I jumped at the opportunity.

Every day after getting Dr. Dray settled into his office, we spent time talking about chiropractic philosophy and the body's innate intelligence. He explained that the body is a self-healing organism and that when the nervous system is in proper balance the body heals on its own. I remember Dr. Dray saying, "The power that created the body heals the body. It happens no other way."

My passion was ignited, and I knew that pursuing a career in chiropractic was the right path for me. I majored in Human Biology and applied to the National College of Chiropractic, located in Lombard, Illinois. While in chiropractic school, I met Dr. Rei, an acupuncturist and chiropractor. Dr. Rei helped me appreciate the natural connection between Chinese medicine and chiropractic. It was while studying acupuncture that I first began to understand the true nature of symptoms and the connection between the central nervous system and the body's acupuncture meridians—

the pathways of energy where chi (life force) flows. I learned that the body speaks with symptoms when chi does not flow harmoniously through the meridians.

Upon graduating from chiropractic school, I began working in a multi-disciplinary healthcenter with Dr. Steven Ciolino. Dr. Ciolino was another angel along my journey. He helped me appreciate the work of Dr. George Goodheart, the founder of Applied Kinesiology, and Dr. John Thie, the founder of Touch for Health. Through these practitioners, I learned the intricate connection between the acupuncture meridians and the muscles of the body and how each individual muscle is associated with a complementary acupuncture meridian as well as specific organs of the body. This insight helped me understand the body's functional and mechanical balance.

I did my post-graduate work with Dr. Jon Sunderlage, a renowned chiropractor most noted for his pioneering electro-acupuncture treatments. Dr. Sunderlage created a system of electro-acupuncture based on the work of Dr. Robert Becker, M.D. Dr. Becker, author of *Body Electric* and *Cross Currents*, is known for his research using electricity to facilitate regeneration. Dr. Sunderlage integrated Dr. Becker's work with electro-acupuncture and Chinese medicine to facilitate the body's ability to regenerate. If I had not seen it for myself, I would have never believed the effectiveness of Dr. Sunderlage's work. Even seeing it, it was still hard to comprehend that his patients were able to regenerate fingers after gangrenous, diabetic neuropathies. I shadowed Dr. Sunderlage for two years on a weekly basis. He is an exceptional person, teacher and doctor with a heart as big as a whale.

In 1995, I developed an inguinal hernia, a condition that usually requires surgery. I began treating myself using Dr. Sunderlage's electro-acupuncture system, which initiated the healing process. However, the catalyst that led to my body's rapid healing was meeting Dr. Steve Popkin, who had studied acupuncture with Lord Pandit Professor Dr. Sir Anton Jayasuriya of Sri Lanka, the most renowned holistic physician in the world. Dr. Popkin's treatment consisted of using two needles in specific points of my body. I continued to use these two points as part of my self-treatments. The inguinal hernia healed in record time and without surgery.

Dr. Popkin and I immediately became great friends. He invited me to attend an international conference for holistic healers where Dr. Anton was the featured speaker. The weekend at the international conference was life-changing. In addition to hearing Dr. Anton talk about his work in Sri Lanka, I met Dr. Ralph Alan Dale, an acupuncturist noted for his research and understanding of The Five Elements and holographic body parts. Following the conference, I knew I had to go to Sri Lanka to study.

Dr. Anton headed Medicina Alternativa at the Kalubowila Hospital in Colombo, Sri Lanka, the alternative healing department of the hospital. Calling it the alternative healing department was quite ironic, however, because it was the busiest section of the facility. Students and doctors traveled from around the world to study and train with Dr. Anton. The training was both intense and illuminating. There were twenty students during the time I trained at Kalubowila. We worked seven days a week, between the hours of 8 a.m. and 10 p.m., treating anywhere between 300 to 500 people daily. Everyone was treated for free. The patients were afflicted with every symptom imaginable, including common colds, allergies, Parkinson's disease, kidney disease, diabetes, traumatic injuries, tennis elbow, sciatica, inflammatory bowel disease, schizophrenia, alopecia, cancer and elephantiasis. We treated everyone with natural modalities: acupuncture, chiropractic, cranial-sacral therapy, homeopathy, herbology, laser therapy, homeopuncture, Ayurvedic medicine, essential oils, chakra balancing and bio-geometry with the use of pyramids. Most of the people had phenomenal results.

I was very fortunate to be the only chiropractor working at the hospital during the training. Every musculoskeletal condition was referred to me, and I had the amazing opportunity to get to know Dr. Anton on a personal level. Working with him expanded my perception of the possibilities for helping the human body heal and the integration of so many natural healing modalities unified at one center.

In 1996, I participated in the World Congress of Alternative Medicine. At the Congress I was introduced to lamas, Tibetan monks, shamans, and many other indigenous healers from around the world. These men and women were examples of a long tradition of people who had learned the ways of the universe and both recognized and accepted the infinite potential that human beings have to heal and become whole. I was in awe of the diverse group of people who had traveled from more than sixty countries to participate in the World Congress. There were lectures about every aspect of healing that covered the spectrum, from color therapy and chakras to pranic healing and plant alchemy.

On my journey home from Sri Lanka, I visited Drs. Thomas Bayne and Ingrid Maes in Belgium. Tom ran a chiropractic practice in Oostende with Ingrid and helped to run the largest nutritional company in all of Europe. His specialty was and still is natural healing using whole food nutritional supplements, including herbal botanical products that assist the body with detoxification.

One of the great treasures of Belgium is its chocolate, and I ate several pieces the first day I arrived. I had not had any chocolate during the time I studied in Sri Lanka, and my body responded with a stomachache. Despite not feeling well, I went with Tom and Ingrid to dinner at the home of their friend, Dr. Philippe Lanckreit. After dinner, Philippe told me he could get rid of the stomachache. Although I did not tell him what I had eaten, within minutes of using a healing modality called Total Body Modification (TBM), Philippe not only told me that my body was having a reaction to chocolate, but the stomachache was gone. I was very excited by the experience and asked Philippe several questions. After explaining the process, he encouraged me to study with Dr. Victor Frank, the developer of TBM, noting that it was the key to understanding "the root of healing."

Shortly after returning to the United States, I sought out and began studying TBM. Over the course of six years, I studied TBM with great enthusiasm and became very close with Dr. Frank. I still consider him a second father. Dr. Frank has worked tirelessly to share with the world TBM's incredible power for healing the body. He is a living testament to the power and efficacy of the treatment. Dr. Frank has used TBM treatments to confront and defy death multiple times.

In 1997, I returned to Sri Lanka to continue my training and to participate in the World Congress of Alternative Medicine for a second time. I introduced TBM to the healers and doctors in the congress and received wonderful feedback.

Incorporating the knowledge I had acquired from my diverse training, TBM became the catalyst for my awakening. Every year at TBM research seminars, where holistic physicians from around the world gathered and shared what they had discovered, I presented what I had learned from synthesizing my knowledge and developing treatments for the people that came to me with health challenges. I received multiple awards for these presentations and acknowledgement of how the techniques I taught were helping people throughout the world.

It was through TBM that I met Dr. Scott Walker, the developer of Neuro-Emotional Technique (NET). I attended many of Dr. Walker's seminars and his work has helped me understand the relationship between emotions and symptoms.

My first major test since being introduced to the many disciplines of holistic medicine was disguised as a mass in my left testicle. Despite the negative thoughts that filled my mind I held true to the belief that every symptom and challenge is an opportunity for change and healing. I was determined to discover the meaning of why my body developed a mass within my testicle and to do whatever it took to heal.

Dr. Frank recommended that I go and see Bob Warwick, a man that has been nicknamed "The Wizard." Bob became my mentor and friend, further expanding the doors of my mind. My body resorbed the mass completely, on its own and without surgery. It took approximately one year. I continued to study and train with Bob for the next three years. I now know why he is called the wizard.

Ultimately, my journey to discover the true *cause* of symptoms began as a child. My journey through the darkness of health challenges took me around the world to study with some of the greatest minds in holistic healing. My studies, experiences and working with countless patients culminated in my awakening to the power of Infinite Love & Gratitude. The process, including the how and why the dots connect, is explained in detail in this book.

The use of the words Infinite Love & Gratitude as a healing modality is both new and revolutionary. It is called The LifeLine Technique and it not only pinpoints and corrects the *source* of imbalance in the body that manifests as symptoms, disease or personal challenges—the internalized, denied or disconnected emotions stored in your subconscious mind—it helps the body heal. Many times the results are *immediate.* From releasing old traumas and embracing life with passion, to creating optimal health and increasing your potential for wealth, opening your heart to the power of Infinite Love & Gratitude will provide you with all the resources and tools necessary to achieve optimal well-being.

To some people, these claims may seem blasphemous. I understand. During the course of my study and the results of my own work with patients, there have been times that the outcome of the treatment so defied the traditional medical paradigm that it was soul-shaking. Nevertheless, I have continued this effort because the actual *proof* was in the results. The health and well-being of thousands of people have been transformed. Let me share with you a few of their stories:

Jake, who is in his late forties, was diagnosed with diabetes. He was prescribed insulin, and as soon as he began to take it, he started to lose his vision. He underwent multiple laser surgeries for his eyes to slow or reverse the retinal damage that had occurred. Unfortunately, the surgeries were unsuccessful, and Jake was diagnosed legally blind. After a month of treatments, his blood sugar metabolism was perfectly balanced and he no longer needed to take insulin. Jake's eyes have begun to regenerate and he is now able to drive during the day. He has been off insulin for three years.

Sharon, a woman in her early thirties, had seen multiple fertility specialists to help her discover why she and her husband were not able to conceive. After five years of fertility tests, medications and psychological trauma, Sharon was feeling hopeless and frustrated. Within two months of treatments, Sharon became pregnant. She now has two beautiful children. I have been blessed to help nearly fifty couples have children; couples who were told that they were infertile.

Lana, age thirty-five, suffered with chronic depression her entire life. Despite years of psychotherapy and taking a variety of anti-depressants, nothing lifted away the gray cloud above Lana's head. The treatments enabled Lana to release the subconscious roadblocks that were at the root of the physical and emotional pain she was feeling. Using The Five Basics for Optimal Health—water, food, rest, exercise and owning her power—Lana is now empowered with the tools to live a life of joy and gratitude. Lana now realizes that she is not a victim of depression—depression was the way her body communicated to let her know that she had disconnected from her truth.

Phyllis, a woman in her late forties, had been suffering with a severe case of psoriasis since she was nineteen years of age. She had attempted to cure it by using many different forms of medication and natural medicine. But nothing seemed to help this very uncomfortable skin condition. By using The LifeLine Technique, we determined why her body was *communicating* with the symptom of psoriasis and corrected the imbalance. In less than a year, Phyllis's skin had healed 95 percent.

Liam, a newborn baby of two weeks, had an extremely traumatic birth. The doctors used metal forceps to remove him from his mother's womb and his brachial plexus (the nerves in his neck that travel into the arms) were torn. Liam was unable to lift his left arm or turn his head. His mother brought Liam to my office after consulting with a neurosurgeon. The neurosurgeon had told her Liam would need multiple surgeries to correct the damage from the injury, but her child would still remain permanently disabled. Within two months of being treated, Liam healed without ever needing surgery. The only remnant of Liam's traumatic birth is a slight winging of his left scapula.

Arlene, a woman in her late sixties, was challenged with macular holes in both of her eyes, a condition that is self-limiting and results in blindness. After three weeks of treatments, her ophthalmologist stated that the macular holes had healed 100 percent.

Jodi, another woman in her late forties, had lost her will to live. She had been severely abused physically and sexually by family members when she was a child. She coped with the emotional and sexual trauma by cutting herself. She used the pain of cutting to numb and cover up the severe pain of her childhood experiences. Because of the horrifying memories, she would not allow herself to become involved in an intimate relationship. Since being treated, Jodi no longer has thoughts of cutting herself. Not only is she no longer haunted by the trauma of her childhood, she has been in a healthy relationship for the past two years.

Every day I experience miracles like these; I witness the transformations of people as they discover how their subconscious thoughts, feelings and limiting beliefs have impeded their ability to heal or achieve greatness. Infinite Love & Gratitude is the key to unlocking the subconscious prison that has trapped us for far too long. Once the portal is open, we are free to soar; free to embrace our unlimited potential and live healthy, fulfilling lives.

My ultimate goal in writing this book is to teach and empower people. More important, I believe it is my moral obligation to share the simplicity and profundity of the power of Infinite Love & Gratitude so that we can all heal our lives and thus create a more peaceful world.

Thank you in advance for joining me on this journey.

With Infinite Love & Gratitude,
Dr. Darren R. Weissman

Introduction

The World is No Longer Flat

It has only been five years since the beginning of the twenty-first century, hailed as a new dawn for humanity. And yet, these are paradoxical times. From the catastrophe of war, terrorism, pestilence, disease and pollution, to the extinction of many forms of life on the planet, we have become eyewitnesses to the greatest changes and challenges humankind has ever faced. We can no longer pretend that the world is the same. Our perception—the way we experience our environment—is forcing us to look around with wide, open eyes.

This transition is not without precedent. In 1491, most people believed the earth was flat. Anyone who sailed a ship into the sunset, it was thought, would likely reach the end of the world and tumble into the depths of hell. That perception changed in 1492 when Christopher Columbus discovered the New World and that the earth was actually round. What a difference one year can make!

Think about Isaac Newton. An apple fell on his head and he wondered, "Why did that happen?" He discovered the law of gravity. Sometime later, Galileo discovered other aspects of gravity, such as the different rates of speed at which objects fall and the impact of wind resistance.

Perhaps a better, more accurate word than "discovered" is *awakened*. The law of gravity existed before Newton and Galileo, just like the New World existed before Columbus arrived.

With a new awareness of gravity, people began to look to the sky and see birds in a different way. They began to fold paper in unique configurations, creating objects that could float in the air. Their perception changed. They *awakened.* Human beings, they realized, had the potential to fly, so they made wing-shaped contraptions and began jumping off cliffs, some to their deaths. Everyone called them crazy. But after many disasters, the Wright brothers developed the Flyer 1 at Kitty Hawk, North Carolina, and took to the skies. In December of 1903, Orville and Wilbur changed the course of humankind by awakening to the potential of powered flight. Think about it! It has only been a little more than 100 years since the famous flight of the Flyer 1. The brothers did not realize at the time that they were learning what the birds already knew: the law of aerodynamics, the right combination of velocity, lift and pressure corresponds with the ability to fly (or crash).

It was Albert Einstein's *awakening* to the theory of relativity, "$E=mc^2$," that has become the bridge between modern day physics and what we now call energy healing, upon which The LifeLine Technique is based. Albert Einstein was seeking to understand the gravitational force on a falling object when he *awakened* to the theory of relativity. "E" refers to energy; "m" defines mass; and "c" is the speed of light. The closer a mass moves towards the speed of light, the greater the gravitational pull and density on that mass. Einstein's theory states that if the mass does not have enough potential energy to reach the speed of light, then the gravitational pull and the density on that mass causes it to stop. However, when the mass reaches the speed of light, it is converted into energy.

The science of quantum physics further demonstrates that everything in the universe is composed of energy and is always in motion. The varying states of matter—solid, liquid and gas—represent the different frequencies of energy. The rate at which energy moves determines the physical state of matter. How life flows through us determines the nature of the flow of energy through the body.

There is a pinnacle law, like the law of aerodynamics that reinforces Einstein's theory of relativity and quantum physics. It is The LifeLine Law of Transformation and Creation: *Emotions transform energy; energy creates movement; movement is change; and change is the essence of life.* The body is very much like a computer—it responds in a binary (turn on, turn off) manner. Every time you experience an emotion, your brain produces an electrical frequency that instantly sends signals and patterns throughout its mass, as well as to every cell in your body. Depending upon the positive, negative, pessimistic or optimistic content of that emotion, its vibratory frequency creates movement or blocks movement within your physical body. Consequently, the direction of your health is dependent upon the unfettered flow of energy to and from the mind. The challenge is that 98 percent of the mind is subconscious. *When life experiences move freely through the subconscious mind, the body is able to heal.*

It is interesting to note the connection between physics and linguistics and how they segue to help us understand the process of healing. Energy in motion is literally e-motion. How the body is transformed by emotions depends upon the regenerative or degenerative cycle in which it expresses itself—a cycle of health or a cycle of disease. The trillions of cells that form the body are constantly breaking down and re-building in a circadian rhythm. This process is called life. In order to heal, light or energy must be able to flow through the physical body unimpeded. As in Einstein's theory of relativity, when energy or light flows through the body, the density or gravitational pull on the body increases. This increase in density forces the body to go through a process of detoxification or purification. The poisons, toxins and blockages that have accumulated over time are released, and now the body is able to regenerate.

Contrary to the allopathic paradigm to symptom relief, it is energy—not pharmaceutical drugs—that promotes the body's self-healing potential. In Chinese medicine, energy or life force is referred to as *chi*. In Ayurvedic medicine, it is referred to as *prana*.

The LifeLine Technique works by balancing the energy of the body to help people release stress and symptoms. Symptoms are a result of stored poisons, toxins or blockages caused by the subconscious internalization, denial or disconnection from emotions. It is by reconnecting to the emotions that have been trapped within the subconscious mind that we can achieve optimal health.

THE NEW FRONTIER OF ENERGY HEALING

Energy healing facilitates the movement of the spirit, creating a more harmonious connection between the body and the universe. The more harmonious your connection is to the universe, the better you will feel, the better your life force will flow. Just as we harness energy from the earth to make our lives easier—from cell phones and satellites to e-mail and television—as human beings we harness energy to both assess and optimize health.

We assess health by measuring the body's electrical potential. Think about it: An electro-cardiogram, or EKG, measures the electrical activity of the heart. When an

EKG is "flat line," the person's body no longer has the potential to maintain its energetic life force, and that person is pronounced dead. The brain's activity is assessed with an electro-encephalogram, or EEG. Muscles are measured with an electro-myelogram, or EMG. It is because of the body's electromagnetic field that we are able to view the different anatomical parts of the body with Magnetic Resonance Imaging, or MRI.

Now take a moment to visualize clouds floating across the sky and waves moving along the surface of water. The energy that pushes the water or the clouds is the same energy that manifests itself within the physical movement of your body. By learning to unleash the blocked energy within your body, you will unlock your infinite potential to achieve optimal health and well-being.

What I know to be true and what the power of Infinite Love & Gratitude and The LifeLine Technique has proven is this: The greatest obstacle to your health and well-being is the subconscious disconnection from your emotions.

LEARNING THE BODY'S LANGUAGE

Paying attention to symptoms is the key to understanding what is going on in your body. Symptoms are the way the body *speaks*. Some symptoms may be quite obvious while others are so subtle you regard them as normal functions. Either way, symptoms are symphonies the body composes to get your attention.

Your body *speaks* only when necessary. Symptoms are the way your body says: "I don't want this in me any longer," or "I'm not happy with the way you are treating me." Your body loves you; it communicates to help you appreciate that you are in danger. I tell all of my patients that symptoms are gifts from the body. These gifts, however, arrive in very strange wrapping paper. Whether the symptoms include headaches, stomach pain, diarrhea, nausea, fatigue, low back pain, depression, panic, anxiety, inflammatory bowel disease, or cancer, they are the body's way of saying, "I am out of balance."

Imbalances in the body occur emotionally, structurally, biochemically or spiritually. When you take a pharmaceutical drug to address a symptom, you are basically telling your body to "shut up," impairing its ability to heal. Emergency medicine is superb for saving lives in times of crisis. However, taking a pill for every symptom inhibits the body's natural ability to heal itself. It is the same as taking the battery out of a fire alarm in your home. Without the battery, the fire alarm cannot alert you to danger. Even worse, the danger escalates. By taking a pill, you mask the body's ability to alert you to danger lurking within.

Emotions can be defined as the energy that moves us. Considering that energy is always in motion, when we internalize, deny or disconnect from an emotion, that energy takes a wrong turn that often keeps us stuck in a maze. Every time internalized, denied or disconnected emotions are triggered, the body becomes compromised and has to compensate, leaving it at risk for injury or opportunistic pathogens. Recurrent symptoms and chronic stress are the warning signs that emotions are trapped within the subconscious mind.

Symptoms start long before we become conscious of them. They usually begin as an uncomfortable feeling. When ignored, that uncomfortable feeling—the emotion that was internalized, denied or disconnected from—manifests in the body as an imbalance. Imbalance in the body leads to stagnation or leakage of life force, resulting in symptoms dependent upon where the stagnation or leakage is located. If left unchecked, the imbalance becomes a pattern of dis-ease and eventually pathology that will devastate the body on every level.

The current medical industry paradigm is to treat and suppress symptoms. For every symptom, your allopathic (medical) doctor is likely to write a prescription for you. Yet, chronic diseases are at an all time high; very few people are getting well. In our nation alone, hypertension, diabetes and obesity are rampant in *every* age group. Not one medication on the market cures these illnesses. Insulin, for example, does not cure diabetes. Doctors never say that chemotherapy, radiation and/or surgery cure cancer. Instead, they say the cancer is in *remission*.

Of course, the doctor's intention is to alleviate the symptoms and help people get well. Many of the medications they prescribe, however, have what doctors refer to as "side effects." I think that is a funny term. They are not "side effects." They are the *direct* effects *caused by the pharmaceutical drugs,* and they create additional symptoms for which you usually are encouraged to take *more medication.* Now you are taking more medication for *symptoms caused by the original medication.* The cycle has spiraled out of control. What happens in the interim? By not listening to what the body was telling you in the first place, you have made it weaker and more vulnerable.

Just remember, nobody knows more about you than you. Nobody sees life through your eyes or hears through your ears or smells through your nose or tastes through your mouth or feels through your skin or is aware of your intuition as acutely as you are. Once you embrace the fact that the natural state of the body is health and wholeness, you will never look at a symptom the same way again. As the late Supreme Court Justice Oliver Wendell Holmes once said, "Man's mind, once stretched by a new idea, never regains its original dimensions." Once you know, you know forever, and that means you must be authentic in how you live your life.

The LifeLine Technique locates the disruption in the flow of energy and releases it immediately, targeting the cause of disease. Sometimes the symptom will go away with one treatment. Other times the process involves a journey to awaken your spirit.

The LifeLine Technique does not work within a vacuum. It requires that you make the *necessary* adjustments in your lifestyle in order to maintain your body's balance. The Five Basics for Optimal Health include the quantity, quality and frequency of water consumption, food intake, rest, exercise, and owning your power. These are the keys to helping the body tap into its innate potential to heal.

YOU CAN HEAL

I know this to be true: You already possess the power and the ability to heal, without medication or pharmaceutical drugs. No matter how serious the illness or how catastrophic the event, the body has the miraculous capacity to regenerate, rejuvenate and revitalize itself. What does it mean to heal? I like the definition written by author Debbie Shapiro in her book, *Your Body Speaks Your Mind:*

> *To heal means to become whole . . . . Becoming whole means bringing all of ourselves into the light, leaving nothing in the dark, no matter how disturbing or painful it may be. It is an embracing of all the parts we have ignored, denied or tried to eliminate. Healing brings all of this into the conscious mind, into our hearts, into our lives.*

When I was a child, the pediatrician told my mother that I had asthma, a condition he said I would have for the rest of my life. The process of treating the asthma included very painful shots all year long for many years, and I was told I had to use bronchial inhalers to prevent asthma attacks. I internalized the belief that being diagnosed with asthma made me weaker than other people. The last asthma attack occurred when I was twenty-two and in chiropractic school. I will never forget struggling to study for an exam while I waited in the emergency room to be administered an adrenaline shot because I was gasping for air. It was the asthma, along with other health challenges, that propelled my journey to become whole. Ultimately, I realized that there is no such thing as a "cure" in the world of allopathic medicine and, if I was going to truly heal myself, I would need to embrace all the parts of myself that I had internalized, denied or disconnected from.

You are your *own* healer. Once you *awaken* to how your subconscious mind impacts your life, coupled with The Five Basics for Optimal Health—quantity, quality and frequency of water, food, rest, exercise and owning your power—your body will be able to create balance and naturally heal itself. The process of healing is a spiritual journey, the evolutionary journey to awakening your spirit. The first step in the journey begins with *choosing* to own your power and to feel.

I have been engaged in an ongoing process of study and practice to help individuals understand the power they already have within themselves to heal from "dis-ease" and to live healthy and fulfilled lives. Through my practice as a holistic physician and doctor of chiropractic healing, I have incorporated multiple traditions and treatment modalities, ranging from the ancient medicine of the barefoot Chinese doctors to the frontiers of energy medicine. These experiences have culminated in *my awakening* to the power of Infinite Love & Gratitude and The LifeLine Technique. The LifeLine Technique corrects the emotional, structural and biochemical imbalances of the body and reconnects the body to the spirit, facilitating the healing process.

Awakening to the power of Infinite Love & Gratitude was akin to understanding that the world was no longer flat and that humankind had the ability to fly. Infinite Love & Gratitude is the connection, the thread that weaves together the complex matrix of the mind, body and spirit. It enables you to embrace the internal matrix that exists in everyone, the matrix that connects you to nature and to the laws of the entire universe.

One person's ability to believe in the power of his or her own imagination can and indeed has changed the course of the planet. Look up in the sky on any given day and you will see airplanes and helicopters. Turn on the news, and you will receive your information via satellite and hear about spacecraft venturing in search of new worlds. All of that is possible because people believed in themselves and their dreams. For those who understand engineering, physics and chemistry, the achievements launched by the Wright brothers' vision may seem quite simple. In many ways, The LifeLine Technique is a product of that simplicity, and that is why it is so effective. It may take some time to master it, but the basic principles of healing are very easy: love, balance and authenticity. Once awakened to The Five Basics for Optimal

Health and The LifeLine Law of Transformation and Creation, the principles are easy for both lay persons and healing arts professionals to comprehend and utilize.

HEALING THE WORLD

I am not a spiritual guru professing *to know the way*. Rather, The LifeLine Technique is part of the continuum of natural healing knowledge that began with the ancient art of Chinese and Ayurvedic medicines. That chain includes Acupuncture, Chakras, Shamanism, Homeopathy, Chiropractic, Applied Kinesiology, Total Body Modification (TBM), Neuro-Emotional Technique (NET), Neuro-Linguistic Programming (NLP), Psychoneuroimmunology, Natural Healing Technique, Eye Movement Desensitization and Reprocessing (EMDR), and many other forms of energy healing. It is based on thousands of years of empiricism, documented research and biomedical evidence.

Along with my colleague and collaborator, Dr. Tom Bayne, my journey toward further development of The LifeLine Technique continues. At our health center, The Way to Optimal Health, we have successfully treated the energy imbalances of thousands of people in a clinical environment, leading them on a path to balance and healing. I believe it is imperative to teach people how to take full responsibility for their lives and heal themselves. My goal is to enable you to understand the language your body uses to communicate and to empower you with healthy lifestyles. My mission is to help heal the world, one person at a time.

The LifeLine Technique enhances the current paradigms of allopathic and holistic medicine. It is the key to restoring the health and vitality of everyone. It is the key to both imagining and creating a world full of awareness, health, respect and love. It is the key to *our awakening* to the magnificent and unlimited capacity we possess as human beings. It is the bridge to a bright future.

During their first treatment, people who are referred to my office often display the attitude: "I'm here, but I'm a skeptic." I like skepticism; I believe it is healthy. Skepticism means you are at least open. It means you will ask questions; you won't follow simply because someone tells you to; you will more than likely pay attention to your gut. No matter what, you will make your own decision.

I encourage you to approach this book with skepticism. But once you read this book, once you witness the phenomenal power of Infinite Love & Gratitude and The LifeLine Technique, you will know that you have unlimited options for healing and that your world will never again be flat.

Part One

The Awakening

Whispers from above, beyond,
beckoning the heart that sighs
lost in slumber, gaining strength
from the mires now to rise,
first a breath, then to see
all that one was meant to be
has always been,
though in disguise, now the Light to realize,
then resonates my soul to sing
. . . . it's time for the Awakening.

Ranel Gretebeck

CHAPTER ONE

Awakening

Looking back, I realize that each experience, each teacher, everything I studied ultimately played a part in awakening to the power of Infinite Love & Gratitude. Each modality I learned and used provided a piece of my personal puzzle: How could I best help the people I treated? Based on what I already knew, the patients I treated made progress. However, there was still something missing.

During the summer of 1998, my cousin Rob Morgan worked as an intern in my office in preparation to become the first deaf chiropractor ever to graduate from the Palmer College of Chiropractic. After a full day of observing my work with patients, Rob turned to me and held up his hand in what I was later to learn meant "I Love You" in sign language. I was amazed by the warm, powerful and peaceful feeling I experienced as Rob held up his hand in the "I Love You" sign. Intrigued by my internal feeling, I asked Rob to hold his arm up as I assessed different reflex points on his body using a muscle test. Depending upon what is being tested, a muscle test uses an indicator muscle to evaluate the balance or integrity of the body. When the muscle becomes weak upon being pressed, it is a signal that there is an imbalance present within the body or its integrity is being compromised.

When I found a weak reflex point, I held my hand in the "I Love You" sign mode next to his body. The reflex in Rob's arm instantly became stronger. I did not realize then the impact of that moment. It would take another three years for all the pieces to fall into place. The missing link, to my amazement, that eventually tied it all together came via e-mail.

I logged on to the Internet to check e-mail. There was a message from my friend, Greg. In the subject line, Greg wrote: "This is going to fascinate you." The message said: "Darren, of everyone I know, I thought you would appreciate this the most." I clicked on the URL at the bottom of the message. A picture of a crystal, one of the most delicate and uniquely formed that I had ever seen, popped up on my screen.

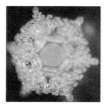

Love and Gratitude

I studied the photo for a long time, drawn to the intricacies of its core and the brilliance of its facets. Even on the computer screen, it seemed to twinkle. It was the work of Dr. Masaru Emoto, a doctor of alternative medicine and a visionary researcher based in Japan. Dr. Emoto had made an amazing discovery:

> *Human vibrational energy—thoughts, words, ideas and music—affects the molecular structure of water. It is the very same water that comprises over 70 percent of a mature human body and covers the same amount of our planet. Water is the very source of all life on this planet; its quality and integrity is vitally important to all forms of life. The body is very much like a sponge and is composed of trillions of chambers called cells that hold liquid. The quality of our life is directly connected to the quality of our water.*

For more than a century, scientists and researchers have been seeking to understand the *true* nature of water and its value for living beings. Naturalist and scientist Johanne Grander was one of the first to note that water is like a liquid tape recorder, storing information and vibratory frequencies. Victor Schauberger's research took it a step further, revealing that water in its natural living state moves with a spiraling, or vortex, action. This vortex action gives water its vitality or "livingness."

Dr. Emoto built upon existing knowledge about water's capacity and capability. He demonstrated not only its vitality, but also how environment affects its *molecular structure*. Using a dark field microscope that had photographic capabilities, he documented his work in his monumental book, *Messages from Water*. Dr. Emoto conducted numerous series of experiments in which he froze samples of water in vials, extracting some of the frozen crystals and examining them under a dark field microscope, where he photographed his results.

In his first samples of the water from different cities in Japan, Dr. Emoto found tremendous discrepancies.

 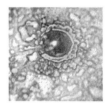

Spring Water   Polluted Lake

The crystals from heavily polluted water were distorted and random, while water from pristine mountain streams and springs showed beautifully formed geometric designs in crystalline patterns. Based on his initial findings, Dr. Emoto decided to expose the water to sound, using Mozart, Bach, Beethoven, Kawachi folk music and heavy metal music.

Mozart's "Symphony   Bach's   Beethoven's
40 in G Minor"   "Air for G String"   "Pastorale"

 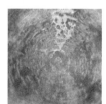

Kawachi Folk Music   Heavy Metal Music

Once again, he was astounded to discover how water responded *differently* to each of the sounds.

Following this series of experiments, Dr. Emoto and his team of researchers examined how thoughts and words affected the formation of untreated, distilled water crystals. He typed words onto paper and then taped them onto glass bottles. The

Distilled Water

bottles were frozen. The next day, water crystals were extracted, examined under a dark field microscope and photographed. **Once again, Dr. Emoto's results showed variation in the formation of each and every crystal, depending upon the words used.**

Love and Gratitude	**Thank You**	**Beautiful**
You Make Me Sick I Will Kill You	**You Fool**	**Dirty**

In another group of experiments, Dr. Emoto's team of researchers placed water on a table. Seventeen participants stood in a circle around the table, holding hands. Each participant spoke a beautiful word of his or her choice to the water, such as "unity," "love" and "friendship." The team took before and after photographs of the water crystals. Not only did the crystals change, the team was excited to discover, but the results were instantaneous.

Tap Water Before   **Tap Water After**
Positive Intention   **Positive Intention**

Dr. Emoto's work provides tangible evidence that thoughts, words, ideas and sound affect the molecular structure of water. He has demonstrated how easily water takes on the vibrations and/or the energy of its environment. Moreover, his study documents that the effects are immediate. Because our bodies are 75 to 90 percent water, his research documents that our bodies are extremely sensitive to emotions, thoughts, the music we listen to and the food we eat. I knew immediately that Dr. Emoto's research had tremendous implications for understanding the emotional, structural, biochemical and spiritual well-being of the human body.

I forwarded copies of the e-mail to my colleague, Dr. Tom Bayne, and printed one for the office, so that our patients could read it while they waited for an appointment. As I was to discover, Dr. Emoto's work was the missing link for which I had been searching.

Building upon existing holistic models, I had already awakened to a wide range of natural healing techniques to address the emotional, biochemical, structural and spiritual components of health. I have always been able to enhance healing on an energetic level using minimal information. Many times at public presentations, I was asked when I was going to merge all of the techniques to which I had awakened into one comprehensive system.

When Dr. Bayne and I first began to collaborate at The Way to Optimal Health, we spent endless hours of our free time brainstorming in an effort to find or create what we knew was out there somewhere, *the* key to helping people truly heal their lives. Each innovation brought us closer, but we were at a loss as to what would unlock the giant steel door to the technique that would profoundly improve the quality of people's lives.

During dinner with Tom, his wife Ingrid, and my then-fiancée Sara, the answer emerged.

"Well?" asked Ingrid.

"Well, what?" responded Tom.

"So what's the new technique?" she said. "You've been at it for months now. Tell us about it."

Tom and I looked at each other like two puppies caught chewing a new shoe.

"Not yet," I said.

"We're still working on it," Tom added.

"Can I be honest with you, Darren?" Ingrid asked.

"Yeah, of course," I replied.

"I think the reason you haven't come up with the technique is because you're just too scared of how powerful it will be."

I will never forget that moment. We all looked at her. The only thing I could do was nod my head.

Later that night, I paced the floor of my home and talked to Sara. Over and over, I could hear Ingrid's voice in my head saying: "You're just too scared." This will sound mystical, but I know of no other way to describe what happened next. One minute I was talking to Sara and the next, the room suddenly froze. I could hear Sara's voice, but I could no longer make out her words. It was as if the top of my head opened and a surge of energy ringed it, sending shivers from my brain down to my arms and fingers. My hands felt tingly, then numb.

"I need a pen and paper," I suddenly yelled to Sara. "Hurry, babe. I think I've got it!"

Within minutes, I drew lines, made circles and wrote words without saying anything. Sara would later tell me that when I finished, I looked so calm and peaceful that my face was iridescent.

"Will you let me use it on you?" I asked, looking up from the paper where I had just scribbled what was to be called The LifeLine Flow Chart.

Sara had been having neck pain for quite a while. I asked her to pinpoint the pain and describe it on a scale of one to ten. I told her to hold her arm at a 90-degree angle from her body to do muscle testing, and then I began to go through the flow chart. Every time Sara's arm went weak I would hold my hand in the "I love you" sign and say the words, "Infinite Love & Gratitude." The pain in Sara's neck changed locations and decreased in intensity. I ran the flow chart again. Minutes later the pain was gone.

"What *is* that?" Sara asked in amazement.

"I'm not sure," I responded. "It came through me like a lightening bolt. I just know this is *it!*"

Although I didn't have any symptoms myself, I decided to run the flow chart on myself, using Sara as a surrogate for muscle testing. When I finished, I felt strong, clearheaded and focused. There was a powerful energy running through my body.

The next day at the office, I sequestered Dr. Bayne to explain the flow chart before we saw our first patients. I knew I was standing at the threshold. Tom was very excited and ready to use it, but I first wanted to see how the morning patients responded. I promised to report back to him after lunch. I saw twenty patients that morning with a multitude of issues, including a sinus infection, colds, neck pain, fatigue, headache, knee pain, and a woman with a panic attack. Everyone responded instantly, leaving the office that day virtually symptom-free.

After finishing with the morning patients, I taught Tom the technique. For the rest of the day, and in subsequent weeks, we used the flow chart as our primary modality for rebalancing the energy in our patients' bodies. We compared notes and continued to modify and refine the flow chart every time we learned something new. Within a week, our office manager designed The LifeLine Flow Chart in the computer.

The moment The LifeLine Flow Chart channeled through me, I realized that every system of natural medicine I had previously studied was actually just a piece of the puzzle. The LifeLine Flow Chart was the missing thread necessary for weaving all of the pieces together into a unified system of healing. But more than just a systematic approach, The LifeLine Flow Chart provides the narrative for explaining what is *really* going on by translating the language of the body and subconscious mind—symptoms—into simple and accessible information that can be used to heal.

Since first awakening to the power of Infinite Love & Gratitude, I have treated thousands of patients and have, along with Dr. Bayne, taught this technique to hundreds of people around the world. Every single day, I learn something new, and that is part of the beauty and wonder of the treatment. The moment one door is opened there is another one behind it. I am humbly honored to be both a trailblazer and a witness.

I wrote this book from both perspectives. My goal is to share with you the philosophy behind every aspect of The LifeLine Technique—from the independent and interdependent mechanism of each system, to how they harmoniously and completely unite to balance the mind, body and spirit. Throughout the book I will share different examples of treatments using The LifeLine Technique and the *subconscious* story behind the symptoms each patient experienced. Some of this information will be viewed as heretical or even blasphemous. However, keep in mind, from the shape of our planet to man's ability to walk on the moon, every revolutionary idea that has changed the course of human history has been met with skepticism, denial and cries of heresy.

Each aspect of **The LifeLine Flow Chart** will be addressed in greater detail throughout the entire book. However, I want to begin by providing you with an overview. The first tier of The LifeLine Flow Chart involves symptoms. Symptoms, which are fully explained in Chapter 8, are the way the body *speaks*. The sole purpose of a symptom is to notify you that you have subconsciously disconnected from an experience. A symptom may be pain or dysfunction anywhere in the body. It may be an uncomfortable feeling when you are around certain people. It may occur when you are giving a speech, driving on the highway, eating a new food or doing anything outside of your comfort zone. But rather than being an obstacle, symptoms are perhaps your greatest benefit. You will learn why as you read this book.

All symptoms occur because there is an imbalance somewhere in the body. That imbalance originates in what is called the **Triad of Health**.

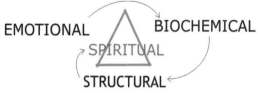

EMOTIONAL   BIOCHEMICAL

SPIRITUAL

STRUCTURAL

The Triad represents the emotional, biochemical, structural and spiritual aspects of the body. The body actually begins to leak or lose life force or energy when an imbalance is present. It is that loss of life force that triggers the body to speak with a symptom. The symptom is the door or portal through which we *discover* what our subconscious mind is saying, and in this light, it is also the means for reconnecting to our truth.

The *root cause* of imbalance in the Triad of Health, which causes the body to lose energy or leak life force, is located in the **Power Center**.

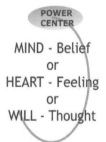

POWER
CENTER

MIND - Belief
or
HEART - Feeling
or
WILL - Thought

Consciously, imbalance begins subtly. However, on a *subconscious* level, imbalance occurs when life experiences create emotional chaos. At that point it is common that we disconnect from our conscious mind, the **Power Center**—your thoughts (will), feelings (heart) or beliefs (mind). The brain automatically and subconsciously internalizes the chaos and keeps the emotions of that experience trapped in a cycle of disconnection.

Like a metal detector, The LifeLine Technique zeroes in on the location of the imbalance in the body and its cause. Secondly, it helps you reconnect to the emotions that you have subconsciously disconnected from so that your body can regain balance and heal.

The **Five Elements** demonstrate the flow of life force through the body's twelve major acupuncture meridians.

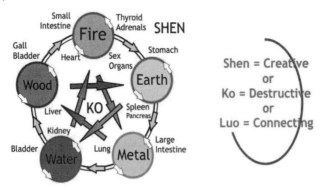

The **Meridians** are a complex matrix of circuits, which provide energy throughout the body and connect us to the universe that we are all a part of. Because emotions are *energy in motion,* blockages within the acupuncture meridians are caused when we are in a state of subconscious disconnection. Blockage anywhere along the meridian pathway causes the body to respond with symptoms. It is by restoring balance within the meridians that the body is able to heal on its own. The Five Elements guide The LifeLine Technique practitioner in the discovery of the exact location of that blockage of life force. The Five Elements help us appreciate and view the subtle connection between the macrocosm of the universe and the microcosm of the body.

The **Expression Channel** explains *why* there is a decrease flow of life force through the acupuncture meridians.

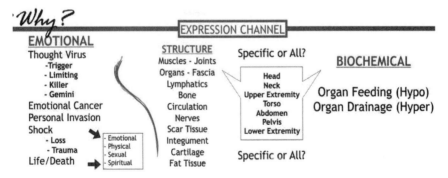

Expression literally means to speak what one is feeling or thinking. The Expression Channel is the body's way of communicating what is going on emotionally, structurally or biochemically. For example, a patient comes to my office with a stiff neck. Traditionally, it has been assumed that a stiff neck might be caused by strained or injured muscles. The Expression Channel of The LifeLine Flowchart, however, provides you with the opportunity to probe even deeper and determine *why* there was a strain or injury in the first place. By running The LifeLine Flow Chart, the patient is able to reconnect to the subconsciously internalized, denied or disconnected emotions that are creating a blockage in his or her acupuncture meridians. When the Expression Channel is cleared, the subconscious emotion is released, increasing the potential for the body to heal effortlessly and completely.

The next step of The LifeLine Flow Chart is to locate the Holding Pattern.

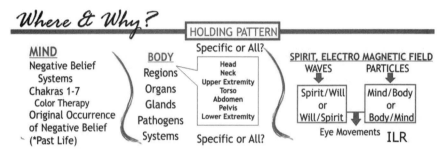

The **Holding Pattern** answers the questions *where* and *why*. *Where* is the holding pattern that is inhibiting the person from becoming conscious and *why* are they not able to release it? The Holding Pattern can be discovered in the mind, the body or the spirit. If the Holding Pattern is located in the mind, it is the result of limiting beliefs inhibiting the person from perceiving the infinite potential and possibilities that exist in every moment. If the Holding Pattern is located in the body, it is due to long standing subconscious disconnections that have resulted in a mutation or physical breakdown of a specific region, organ, gland, pathogen or system. If the Holding Pattern is in the spirit or electromagnetic field of the body, it is due to a trauma that is sustaining a disconnection between the spirit and will or the mind and the body. This disconnection is associated with the eyes and the inability for the eyes to process trauma during REM sleep. When the Holding Pattern is located, the body releases the grip of limiting beliefs, physical body disconnection, or trauma, which enables the body to heal. Releasing the subconscious emotions that are stuck in a holding pattern enables a person to create a new view towards life's challenges, overcome addiction and reconnect to their truth.

The LifeLine Flow Chart next guides the practitioner to the **Assemblage Point**— the specific anatomical location within the microcosmic orbit (superconscious) where a person originally disconnected within their subconscious mind, thus creating the attractor field for the symptom or challenge.

By locating the Assemblage Point, the practitioner, in a shamanic-type fashion, is able to seal the leaks in the patient's energetic field or *reassemble* the electromagnetic field of the body.

Once we reconnect to the emotions of the subconscious mind, it is necessary to assess the lifestyle changes the person needs to make.

Water, Food, Rest, Exercise, Own Your Power

It is of utmost importance that the body is nurtured and nourished so that it is healthy enough to integrate and conduct its life force. The LifeLine Flow Chart will, like a laser, guide you through the journey of discovery and of understanding the root cause of every symptom or stressful situation. This book is the map, complete with descriptions explaining every road upon which you will travel.

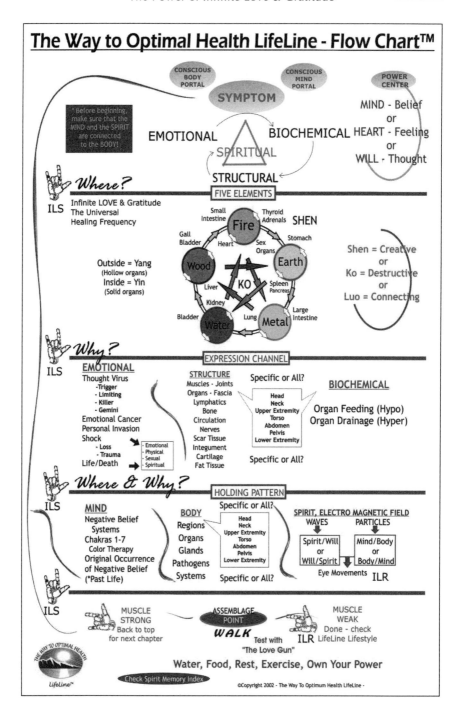

The Way to Optimal Health LifeLine - Flow Chart™

CONSCIOUS BODY PORTAL

CONSCIOUS MIND PORTAL

POWER CENTER

SYMPTOM

MIND - Belief
or
HEART - Feeling
or
WILL - Thought

EMOTIONAL   BIOCHEMICAL

SPIRITUAL

* Before beginning, make sure that the MIND and the SPIRIT are connected to the BODY!

STRUCTURAL

FIVE ELEMENTS

Where?

ILS

Infinite LOVE & Gratitude
The Universal
Healing Frequency

Small Intestine

Thyroid Adrenals SHEN

Fire

Gall Bladder   Heart   Sex Organs   Stomach

Outside = Yang
(Hollow organs)
Inside = Yin
(Solid organs)

Wood   Earth

Liver   KO   Spleen Pancreas

Kidney

Shen = Creative
or
Ko = Destructive
or
Luo = Connecting

Bladder   Lung   Large Intestine

Water   Metal

Why?

ILS

EXPRESSION CHANNEL

EMOTIONAL
Thought Virus
-Trigger
- Limiting
- Killer
- Gemini
Emotional Cancer
Personal Invasion
Shock
- Loss
- Trauma
Life/Death

- Emotional
- Physical
- Sexual
- Spiritual

STRUCTURE
Muscles - Joints
Organs - Fascia
Lymphatics
Bone
Circulation
Nerves
Scar Tissue
Integument
Cartilage
Fat Tissue

Specific or All?

Head
Neck
Upper Extremity
Torso
Abdomen
Pelvis
Lower Extremity

Specific or All?

BIOCHEMICAL

Organ Feeding (Hypo)
Organ Drainage (Hyper)

Where & Why?

ILS

HOLDING PATTERN

Specific or All?

MIND
Negative Belief
Systems
Chakras 1-7
Color Therapy
Original Occurrence
of Negative Belief
(*Past Life)

BODY
Regions
Organs
Glands
Pathogens
Systems

Head
Neck
Upper Extremity
Torso
Abdomen
Pelvis
Lower Extremity

Specific or All?

SPIRIT, ELECTRO MAGNETIC FIELD
WAVES   PARTICLES

Spirit/Will   Mind/Body
or   or
Will/Spirit   Body/Mind

Eye Movements   ILR

ILS

MUSCLE
STRONG
Back to top
for next chapter

ASSEMBLAGE
POINT

WALK

Test with
"The Love Gun"

MUSCLE
WEAK
Done - check
ILR LifeLine Lifestyle

THE WAY TO OPTIMAL HEALTH

LifeLine™

Check Spirit Memory Index

Water, Food, Rest, Exercise, Own Your Power

©Copyright 2002 - The Way To Optimum Health LifeLine -

CHAPTER TWO

The Fusion of Science and Spirit

Two weeks after treating our patients, using what we now called The Life-Line Technique, I suggested to Tom that we conduct a live blood cell analysis of one of our patients both before and after a LifeLine treatment. We used a dark field microscope, the same type of microscope that Dr. Emoto used to conduct his experiments on water. The patient I had in mind was a man who had been diagnosed with Hepatitis C. Tom took a sample of the patient's blood and looked at it under the dark field microscope. The sample revealed severe liver distress; the man's red blood cells were sticking together and not moving. His blood sample displayed signs of lymphatic congestion and abnormal amounts of white blood cells, unhealthy in shape and function. We observed the slide for twenty minutes and then returned to the patient to perform The LifeLine Technique.

It took less than ten minutes to run The LifeLine Flow Chart, after which we drew blood again. We stared at the slide, astonished by the results. The patient's blood had undergone a complete transformation! All of his red blood cells were now moving freely and were perfectly spaced and shaped. The lymphatic stagnation had cleared up. All of the pathogenic imbalances that were initially present had improved.

"That's incredible!" I said to Tom. "I think we're on to something."

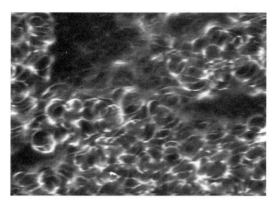

Blood Before LifeLine Treatment

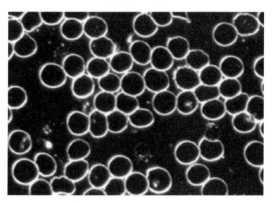

Blood After LifeLine Treatment

Dr. Emoto's work provided that water's molecular structure is impacted by every aspect of its environment. In his word and crystal experiments, the most intricately formed crystal was extracted from the frozen vial on which the words "love" and "gratitude" were taped. The link to health with this experiment is the fact that the human body is 75 to 90 percent water. In one moment, all of the pieces of the puzzle fused into a beautiful image. I immediately understood the impact of the experience I had three years earlier with my cousin Rob. All of Rob's water molecules, which make up each cell of his body, responded to the vibrational frequency of love when I held the "I love you" sign next to his body. The autonomic reflex of the muscle test improved as the water molecules transformed. It was a moment of clarity. I had transcended a belief and entered the realm of knowing. The energy of Infinite Love & Gratitude has the potential to affect the highest of frequencies, which means it has the power to harmonize the body and help it restore balance.

As human beings, the molecular structure of water in our bodies is affected by every experience we encounter. However, most significantly is the subconscious mind's response to the experiences of our life. Subconscious limiting or pessimistic thoughts, feelings and beliefs will result in the stagnation of our cells, eventually leading to symptoms and disease. Remember, 98 percent of our perception is subconscious.

When the words "Infinite Love & Gratitude" are written or spoken, as documented by Dr. Emoto's research with water, these profound words have instantaneous affects on the molecular structure of water—the same water that permeates each cell in the body. Using The LifeLine Technique, Dr. Bayne and I have witnessed and participated in phenomenal healings that we have been able to objectively measure. People who come to our health center or seminars are empowered to take charge of their lives through the use of The LifeLine Technique. The beauty and truth is that healing is all about love and gratitude.

Using live blood cell analysis and a dark field microscope, we have continued to document this phenomenon at The Way to Optimal Health, our center for holistic healing. Instantaneous molecular healing changes have been consistently observed within the blood after Dr. Bayne and I perform The LifeLine Technique. (See Appendix A) One of the greatest results of Dr. Emoto's work and the advent of The LifeLine Technique is the documented and tangible evidence of the healing power of Infinite Love & Gratitude. Why does love heal? That is a question that has withstood the test of time, but now can be answered as a result of Dr. Emoto's work and the diagnostic tests that Dr. Bayne and I have conducted as documentary proof of The LifeLine Technique's effectiveness.

After using The LifeLine Flow Chart, muscle testing, and the words "Infinite Love & Gratitude" on our patient with the Hepatitis C diagnosis, we observed the changes in the molecular structure of his blood. If I did not see it for myself, I would not have believed it! Instant molecular changes had occurred. I am not a Hepatitis C specialist, nor do I treat Hepatitis C. On the contrary, I help people whose bodies are imbalanced and expressing themselves with symptoms. By using The LifeLine Technique and the power of Infinite Love & Gratitude, I am able to help people regain balance in both their mind and body, thus creating the perfect environment for healing to occur. Within a year, the viral load in his body had decreased by more than 90 percent.

As Tina Turner sings, "What's love got to do with it?" Because the body is two-thirds water and water acts as a liquid tape recorder, it is very sensitive to both its internal and external environment. As demonstrated by Dr. Emoto, love and gratitude enhance water's molecular structure and function, thereby enabling the body to release its optimal healing potential.

When the molecular structure of our cells is healthy and intact, the cells better conduct electricity and therefore regulate homeostasis more efficiently. Dr. Bayne and I have documented that when the words "Infinite Love & Gratitude" are spoken or experienced, the molecular structure of the body's cells immediately undergoes a healing change.

Valerie Hunt, author of the book *Infinite Mind*, states, "Theoretically, I accept that the mind is the most powerful force in the world, more powerful than the split atom because it is beyond physical force." The essence of love cannot truly be captured by reading a book. It must be experienced within the mind. The power of the mind and that of love is that they are both one and infinite. To experience the mind and love, all judgement must be released. The power of Infinite Love & Gratitude is an experience—a moment of being present, of defying logic and embracing intuition and the heart.

Helen Keller once said, "The best and most beautiful things in the world cannot be seen or even touched. They must be felt with the heart." It is in each and every moment that we are faced with the ultimate choice; a choice of faith—faith that the universe is a perfect creation and that every moment is a "big bang," a moment of infinite possibilities. In this moment, if I choose to be ruled by fear, what will the consequences be? If I choose to embrace this moment with love and gratitude, what will the consequences be? Your heart knows the difference. It feels each moment that you have disconnected from love and gratitude. Consequently, every fear-driven beat of the heart plays a symphony of victimization and suffering.

Love is a state of openness, the essence of acceptance. The frequency of love amplifies conductance. Conductance literally means movement. Movement, as we know from The LifeLine Law of Transformation and Creation, is change and the essence of life. When we disconnect from love, fear is more apparent. Living in a constant state of fear occurs when we have disconnected from love. In a fearful state, we create boundaries for protection. We create illusionary lines and differences between people, places and things. It is by recognizing that we are all connected through love, and discovering unity within the diversification of life, that the illusionary boundaries begin to melt away.

The following poem, "The Treasure of Love," was composed for my wedding ceremony by my wife's cousin, Kristin Dawson:

Love . . . .
Simple and at times complicated in its expression

Defined over the ages by many,
        No two definitions the same.
The truth of love being found
        By each of us in different ways.

Warmth . . . . Peace . . . . Selflessness . . . . Nurturing . . . .
Guidance . . . . Joy . . . . Comfort . . . . Strength . . . .
Loyalty . . .
Thoughtfulness & Tenderness.
Surrounded by these, you will know Love.

Love is a treasure
        More precious than we can measure.
Too often locked away
        Kept safe, not used.
But the value of love
        Is in the life that it gives
It needs to be shown.
At the core of Love is expression.

Love is both giving and receiving.
More than a feeling . . .
        A decision,
A choice to care for another
        As well as you care for yourself.

Experience Love,
Express it often,
Care for each other,
Enjoy the treasure of Love.

Love is the subtle web that maintains connections. From the beginning of time love has guided and enlightened searchers of the truth. Love is a power that uplifts and transforms people who have lost their will. Love moves the waters and shapes the mountains. Its ethereal nature bonds families, races, species, and potentiates the harmony of all humanity.

One thing an experienced outdoors person knows is never to get caught between a mother bear and her cub! Love causes us to act and react in ways beyond prediction. All life forms—humans, animals and other forms of nature—will do whatever necessary to maintain their connection with love because it is the life force that feeds and nourishes all living beings at their core. Without it we literally die.

The lack of self-love is the final, destructive blow. It results in a lifeless life—a life without passion, reason and ultimately without connection to self or nature. Author Don Miguel Ruiz, a shaman and healer, writes in his book, *The Mastery of Love*:

> *We can talk about love and write a thousand books about it, but love will be completely different for each of us because we have to experience love. Love is not about concepts; love is about action. Love in action can only produce happiness. Fear in action can only produce suffering.*
>
> *The only way to master love is to practice love. You don't need to justify your love; you don't need to explain your love; you just need to practice your love. Practice creates the master.*

Love is a learned behavior. Richard Carlson, Ph.D., once wrote, "Love begins in our own hearts. It is a choice . . . . each choice we make along the way becomes an important step on the path of love." Just as the process of life is the continuum of many experiences, love is the product of fully embracing life's experiences without judgment. Life provides endless resources and opportunities for learning how to master love. It is the choice we make to embrace our magnificence; it is the choice we make, as Don Miguel Ruiz says, to become masters.

The simplest component of The LifeLine Technique is the treatment itself—saying the words "Infinite Love & Gratitude" and holding your hand in the universal sign language hand mode for "I Love You."

You do not need a doctorate, medical degree or holistic health training to perform The LifeLine Technique. Whether you are an executive, nurse, grocery store clerk, salesperson, messenger or a homemaker, once trained in The LifeLine Technique, you will have all of the tools necessary to face any challenge.

For example, a young woman of eighty-three years of age, who had taken just one of The LifeLine Technique training seminars, had an amazing experience. She had been feeling dizzy and even thought she was going to pass out while riding the train. The next morning, she was still feeling dizzy and decided to check her blood pressure. It was 161/85. Her pressure had never before been that high. She treated herself with The LifeLine Technique. The treatment took about fifteen minutes. She took her pressure again. It was 151/75. It had dropped ten points on both the systolic and diastolic pressures, and the dizziness totally went away.

It is my hope that one day this type of training—not just the technique, but also the philosophy of which The LifeLine is a part of the continuum—will become integrated into the school curriculum for children, signaling a profound shift in the way we view symptoms, healing and life.

CHAPTER THREE

Conversations with the Body

Because we have been taught that imbalances such as allergies, hypertension and diabetes are hereditary conditions, we feel as if we are victims of our environment and prisoners of our genes. We believe we do not have any control over illness and disease. The advent of The LifeLine Technique provides a liberating alternative to those beliefs by demonstrating that we have 100 percent control over our health. The first step is to learn to talk to the body.

In 1964, Dr. George Goodheart, Jr., D.C., awakened to Applied Kinesiology (AK), or muscle testing, as a diagnostic and therapeutic tool. He integrated muscle testing into his treatment procedures. Through his ongoing research and the results of his work, Dr. Goodheart discovered the relationship between the body's major muscle groups and the acupuncture meridians.

Many other innovative practitioners expanded upon Dr. Goodheart's original work. Using his powerful intuition, Dr. Victor Frank awakened to and developed Total Body Modification (TBM), a technique that utilizes kinesiology to assess the functional, physiological health of the body. Dr. Frank learned that he could communicate with the body through muscle testing.

Expanding the boundaries of TBM, Dr. Scott Walker awakened to the Neuro-Emotional Technique (NET), a kinesiological way to understand functional, emotional imbalances.

All of these doctors balance the body with kinesiological-based treatments. AK focuses on the structural aspects of the body. TBM focuses on the functional, physiological aspects of the body. NET focuses on the emotional aspects the body. Each of these magnificent techniques overlap with one another in a beautiful mosaic, creating the totality of energetic healing at its best!

The LifeLine Technique uses muscle testing as the diagnostic and therapeutic tool to reveal the root cause of all symptoms. By connecting the emotional, biochemical and structural aspects of the body to the spirit with Infinite Love & Gratitude, The LifeLine Technique facilitates the body's healing process in an extraordinary way.

The LifeLine Flow Chart provides a guided journey through the subconscious mind, helping you to understand how your body manifests what is in your mind. That is why symptoms are a gift. They are the body's way of saying, "The emotions you are internalizing, denying or disconnecting from are hurting me."

Take some time right now to close your eyes and think about a friend. Let whatever emotions about that friend come into your mind. Now, think about when you were in fifth grade. Remember your teacher, the house you lived in, your friends and whatever other memories associated with that time, and let the thoughts just flow. Now, think about your mother and let your mind experience her through whatever thoughts, feelings and beliefs that arise. Open your eyes now and see that your friend, your fifth grade experiences and your mother are not present. However, they still are present in your subconscious mind.

Every emotion that you have ever experienced is imprinted in your mind, whether or not you are aware of it. With The LifeLine Flow Chart and muscle testing, you now have the ability and the power to connect to the subconscious mind and heal it. With this knowledge, there are no limits. Anything and everything is possible.

A landmark study by Dr. Daniel Monti, M.D., et al, measured the effects of cognitive factors on muscle strength and demonstrated the validity of muscle testing. The study conclusively demonstrated how thoughts and statements illicit changes within a muscle test reflex.

The body has an innate intelligence that can be assessed with muscle testing to determine whether it is maintaining balance. Just like the autonomic nervous system, muscle testing is a polarity-dependent mechanism where a muscle will maintain its strength when there is a congruency with the function, adaptability and survival of the entire organism. When there is incongruency with the function, adaptability or survival of the entire organism, an indicator muscle will test weak.

A specific organ, pathogen, system, acupuncture meridian, chakra, muscle, belief, etc., can be used to assess congruence or incongruence through the locking out or giving way of a muscle test. When a muscle locks out, it is an indication that whatever is being tested is congruent with the overall balance of the body. When a muscle gives way, it is an indication that whatever is being tested is incongruent with the overall balance of the body.

The LifeLine Flow Chart, used with muscle testing, enables you to discover the incongruent patterns within the subconscious mind that have manifested as imbalances or symptoms in the body. For example, by touching a painful area of the body, an indicator muscle will sometimes give way, indicating incongruence with the function of that particular area. The LifeLine Flow Chart can then be used with muscle testing to balance those patterns within the subconscious mind that have resulted in the pain or are the result of why the pain has not healed. With muscle testing, The LifeLine practitioner never has to guess. With each question asked, the muscle will either stay locked or give way.

Muscle testing involves the use of an indicator muscle, which is created by extending either the left or right arm at a ninety-degree angle to the body. To assess for a strong reflex, the arm is held in a locked position while the practitioner uses his or her hand to press against it. A good way to test the difference is through the use of a declarative statement. When a person states his or her name, the indicator muscle will remain locked. However, if the person states a name that is not his or hers, the indicator muscle will give way or test weak. For example, if I make the statement, "My name is Darren," the indicator muscle will stay locked. However, if I state, "My name is Jeri," the indicator muscle will test weak. Do this exercise again by placing a package of sugar next to the body. The muscle will instantly become weak because sugar is a poison. The self-preservation mechanism of the body discerns whether a substance is harmful through the strength or weakness of a muscle. Say the word "Love" and an indicator muscle will be strong. Now say the word "Hate" and it will instantly become weak.

For some people it will take some practice to feel the difference between a locked and a weak muscle. Even working with twenty-five to thirty patients daily, it took me about a year before I felt as if I had mastered muscle testing. Once you get the feel for it, however, you will be able to recognize the sometimes subtle differences between a muscle that stays locked and one that gives way.

A surrogate (another person's arm) may be used to evaluate a very young child, an elderly person with disabilities, or anyone who is unable to use his or her own arm. There is no difference between using a surrogate's arm or the patient's own arm during the evaluation. Surrogate muscle testing creates an electrical circuit between the patient and the surrogate. The person performing the muscle testing needs to be focused on the person he or she is testing, not the surrogate.

It is important never to guess while muscle testing! If you are unable to tell the strength or weakness of the muscle, use a surrogate. There are many reasons why a person's muscle may feel "boggy." Usually, it is due to dehydration. During muscle testing, it is imperative that both the tester and the person being tested remain in Present Time Consciousness (focused intent). To stay in tune with the process, have the person being tested resist while muscle testing is performed, so that the strongest muscle possible will be evaluated.

The LifeLine Technique uses muscle testing as a tool to evaluate balance or imbalance and to detect the emotional, structural, biochemical or spiritual source of a symptom. It is the portal through which we communicate with the body and find out what is *actually* going on. Diagnostic tests, such as blood tests and urinalysis, do not show dysfunction until there is at least a *40-plus percent* breakdown in the body. With muscle testing, however, we can determine imbalance within *1 to 2 percent* of dysfunction, which means that you do not need to have a symptom to find a weak muscle. The body's innate intelligence hones in on minute changes before they actually become a significant health challenge.

When there is a change in the indicator muscle—that is, when a strong muscle gives way—it is a signal that an imbalance is present. Using The LifeLine Technique, imbalances are corrected immediately and changes can be observed with the use of muscle testing. The previously weak indicator muscle will test strong immediately after a correction has been made. The simplicity of a correction is saying the words "Infinite Love & Gratitude".

The LifeLine Technique does not *cure* anything. In fact, no "healer" ever *heals*— it is the body that performs the healing process. The healing arts practitioner is like a mechanic who knows the steps necessary to remove any barriers to the smooth running of a car. The intent of the practitioner is vital. A positive attitude, along with a vision of health and love, is imperative while working on someone or on yourself. In addition, it is imperative that you harbor no preconceived notions about whether the muscle will become weak or strong in response to the questions asked. You may be wrong. It is best to let the body's innate intelligence guide you. You will be amazed by the laser-like accuracy that muscle testing reveals.

CHAPTER FOUR

Going with the Flow

Thousands of years ago, Chinese philosophers awakened to the Wu Hsing, or *The Five Element Theory*, which explains the natural flow of the universe. Based on this natural law, everything in the universe has a relationship that is interdependent in some way. These relationships are between the **Five Elements—Fire, Earth, Metal, Water** and **Wood**. The "element" in Chinese means movement and change, which explains the relationships the Five Elements have to each other.

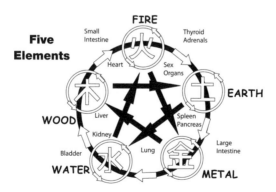

Early philosophers realized that there was a specific pattern that existed between the elements of the universe. Through this observation and their experience, the Five Element Theory was expounded upon to help them understand how human beings maintain balance within themselves and the universe of which they are a part. They observed that the cycle of the seasons was infinite in the expression of life and death. From spring to summer and then from autumn to winter, they realized there was a universal energy that cycled over and over again. It was in this cycle that the mind-body-spirit danced in a symphony of life. The lesson they learned through observation was that nature moved via the law of least effort. Water takes on the form of its vessel. Metal flows like water when heated by fire. Water also has the capacity to extinguish fire. At the same time, if a fire is hot enough it has the ability to evaporate water. The Five Elements are simply intricate and intricately simple.

The Chinese observed that there were three distinct patterns or cycles to how the Five Elements interacted. They called these patterns the **Shen, Ko** and **Luo**. The **Shen** is the creative cycle of nature that each one of the elements naturally created the other in a continuous cycle of life. From fire came the "Big Bang" from which the earth was created. From Mother Earth, when we dig deep within her, we discover precious metals. These metals, when melted, flow like majestic waters. Water when poured onto the earth brings life in the form of trees. When two pieces of wood are rubbed together the friction creates fire beginning the Shen cycle all over again.

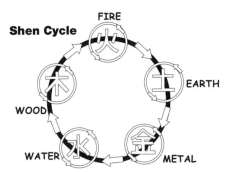

The **Ko** cycle is the controlling or destructive cycle. Beginning with the fire element, a blazing fire will melt metal, as in the process of forging a sword. Metal destroys wood, such as an axe chopping down a tree. Wood controls the earth, such as a tree growing out of the ground. Earth surrounds and controls water, such as a lake or a river. Water controls fire, by extinguishing it, completing the Ko cycle.

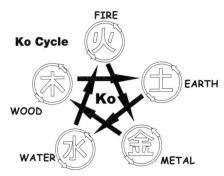

The **Luo** or connecting cycle relates to the principle of yin and yang. In the yin/yang symbol, one half is white and the other half is black. Within the white, there is a small dot of black; within the black, there is a small dot of white. This represents the interdependency of polar opposites. In the Five Element Theory, each element has a yin and yang component as represented by a particular acupuncture meridian. The Luo cycle represents the yin and yang component and demonstrates the interdependence and balance between the acupuncture meridians within an individual element.

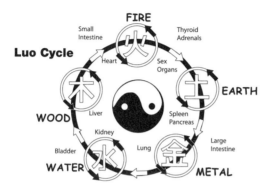

It is within all these cycles that regeneration and rejuvenation occur. From new to old and back to new again, each cycle occurs within a year's time, much like the way a tree forms a new ring. The more balanced a tree, the sturdier and healthier it will be. Whales will migrate, bears will hibernate, caterpillars will transform into butterflies, all with the specific patterns of the Five Elements and the seasons.

Since the dawn of technology, human beings have attempted to control and harness the earth's resources for energy. The results have been catastrophic for the earth and her inhabitants. Destruction of coral reefs, rain forests, holes within the ozone and melting of the polar ice caps are but a few of the obvious consequences. As a result, the destruction of the earth has left the animal kingdom in chaos. For example, the natural migratory patterns of whales have been disrupted causing many whales to beach themselves.

The same chaos occurs within the body when you do not recognize the importance of flowing with the universe rather than against it. Your body appreciates the outdoors and increase of activity and sunlight in the summer, just as it appreciates slowing down and internalizing in autumn and winter. When you deny or disconnect from the natural cycle of the seasons, your body becomes imbalanced, leading to symptoms and disease. The symptoms are the warning signal that you have strayed off course from your natural rhythm. This rhythm is flowing within your acupuncture meridians.

There are twelve pathways of energy or life force within the body called meridians. Each one of these meridians corresponds with an individual organ and carries life force to and from the organ through the meridian. It is literally a network of invisible wires that enable your body to function. These meridians will always show imbalance long before the actual organ has a disease. For example, not everyone who has a gallbladder meridian imbalance has a disease in their gallbladder organ. However, everyone that has a diseased gallbladder has imbalance within the gallbladder meridian. Removing the gallbladder does not correct the imbalance in the meridian; it only removes the diseased organ. The imbalance in the body will persist if the cause of the imbalance in the gallbladder meridian is not addressed. Therefore, maintaining health in your meridians is imperative to insure an optimally healthy life.

Dianne Connelly, Ph.D., wrote a phenomenal book called *Traditional Acupuncture: The Law of the Five Elements.* I read this book at the beginning of every season. It helps me to keep in tune with the natural flow of the seasons. With this awareness, I am able to maintain Present Time Consciousness more efficiently and adapt appropriately to the changes that are occurring.

Life is about change; nothing that lasts ever remains the same. It is easy to get stuck in a pattern of internalization, denial or disconnection. When we do, however, the energy or life force that moves within our meridians becomes affected. It is with the power of Infinite Love & Gratitude that we are able to view our challenges from a new perspective, empowering us to make the necessary changes for both survival and learning.

Your experiences are the treasures of your life. The feelings that result from your experiences will guide you through comfort and discomfort. You must feel to heal. When you are authentic in your expression of your emotions, you will find it easier to go with the flow. It is very simple, though it may be challenging. Have faith in the process. May your spirit move like the wind; may it flow effortlessly like the Five Elements.

CHAPTER FIVE

My, Try, Can't: The Power of Words

"Sticks and stones may break my bones, but words can never hurt me." That is a familiar childhood taunt that we have previously believed to be true. But as we have learned from Dr. Emoto's work, words have an energy frequency that affects the molecular structure of water. Because the body is 75 to 90 percent water, our bodies are affected by words. Words cannot only hurt us emotionally, but the words that we choose to use represent the flow of our subconscious mind.

In 1967, Jennifer was thirteen and excited about being invited to her first teenage party. When she told her friend about the invitation, Jennifer's friend responded, "No boy will ever want to dance with you." At the time of those remarks, Jennifer and her friend were eating tuna salad. When Jennifer began dressing for the party hours after the conversation, her nose and lips began to swell. Her parents took Jennifer to the emergency clinic and the doctor declared her allergic to fish. From that point forward, over the next thirty-five years, Jennifer never ate fish, and if she was around while it was cooking, she had an allergic reaction.

Using the words and intention of "Infinite Love & Gratitude," I harmonized the internalized thoughts, feelings and beliefs associated with Jennifer's memory. She no longer has any allergic reaction to fish and enjoys eating it on a regular basis.

Words can have a profound, life-altering positive impact or can create profoundly negative, devastating affects. Think about the words used when you have a disagreement with your spouse or significant other, when you receive criticism from your parents, or praise from your boss. How do words affect you when your siblings, friends or co-workers tease you? If you do not respond right away, what energy frequencies are rumbling around your body as a result?

Some words that you use everyday have a similar impact. Close your eyes and say the words "my, try and can't." What feelings do those words have for you?

Let us start with the word "my." The word means "belonging to" or "done by me." So what happens when you use the word "my" to describe a symptom or disease? "My migraine headache is killing me." "My allergies are making me sneeze like crazy." "My arthritis won't let me stand up for long periods." "My diabetes is acting up."

When you use the word "my" when speaking of a symptom or a disease, you create an identity as if the symptom or disease defines you. That is dangerous! Adding the word "my" means the symptom belongs to you. The truth is the ache or any other dysfunction is a sign that there is an imbalance in your system and your body is attempting to get your attention. When you qualify the headache by calling it *"my headache"* it sends a negative message to your body and the cycle of breakdown continues. In addition, when you participate in verbal patterns of communication that are pessimistic or limiting in any way, the body has to take on another opponent— you. It is hard to defend against yourself. It is like shadowboxing. The opponent ducks every time you duck.

This is what I recommend: When you talk about a symptom, make it *the* pain instead of *my* pain—*the* pain in my head, *the* pain in my stomach or *the* pain in my back. At the same time, you should own your body parts, i.e., *my* head, *my* stomach or *my* back. Do not say *my* arthritis, *my* multiple sclerosis or *my* Parkinson's disease. When you do, you are just solidifying dysfunction as being a part of you.

Why is this important? The founders of Neuro-Linguistic Programming (NLP), Richard Bandler and John Grinder, have spent their lives studying the impact of language on the nervous system. "Neuro" refers to the mind and the way you externally experience and internally represent the world through your senses. "Linguistics" refers to the use of language with others and yourself. "Programming" refers to the sequence or patterns of your behavior that can be changed, like reprogramming a computer. Bandler and Grinder discovered that language programs the nervous system. And what does your nervous system control? Everything!

Words are powerful. When you speak, you are in effect programming yourself and you will manifest the physical results. Think about what happens when you say: "If you don't put on your hat, you're going to catch a cold," or "You make me sick," or "You always mess up everything."

Bandler and Grinder developed NLP in California during the 1970s, based on their study of three exceptional communicators: the noted family therapist, Virginia Satir; the originator of gestalt therapy, Fritz Perls; and the hypnotherapist, Milton H. Erickson. Bandler and Grinder noted that these communicators were achieving outstanding results with their clients and that they had much in common in the way they related: the language patterns they used, for example, and the beliefs that guided their behaviors. Bandler and Grinder also drew on the work of others to develop a set of beliefs and techniques that allowed them to help people change their lives. There are several core beliefs that are the foundation of NLP. The most commonly referenced are:

❏ **The map is not the territory.**

You respond to *your* map of reality, not reality itself.

❏ **Mind, body and spirit are one system.**

The mind, the body and the spirit are inextricably linked—change one and the others must change.

❏ **Having choice is better than not having choice.**

The greatest number of choices in any interaction provides you with the opportunity to exert the greatest amount of influence over it.

❏ **Excellence can be modeled.**

If one person can do something, anyone can learn to do it.

❏ **All human behavior provides you with an opportunity to create something positive.**

Both positive and negative behaviors create an opportunity for you to learn lessons. What may appear as negative behavior only appears so because you do not yet know, or you have not yet experienced, the positive effect. Behavior is the result of an adaptive positive intent.

❏ **The meaning of communication is the response you get.**

The response may not be the one you intended. If you do not get the result you want, do something different.

❏ **You have all the resources within you to achieve what you want to achieve.**
You have all the resources necessary to make any desired change. No one is wrong or broken.

Based on the theory of NLP, if you say, "I can't do that," you will not be able to do it. The word *can't* is like having your hands and feet bound together behind your back. Short of that, anything is possible. What do you think happens when you act as if these suppositions are true?

You can always do your best. There is no failure, only opportunity. Let me say that again: There is no failure. What our society defines as failure or an obstacle, with all the negative connotations, is actually an opportunity—an opportunity to learn important life lessons and create something positive.

"Can't" is a word that places artificial limitations on yourself, or that other people use to define you. Where would the world be if Albert Einstein listened to his grade school teachers, who told him that he would never do well in science? Where would the National Basketball Association be if Michael Jordan had listened to his high school coaches, who said he would never play pro ball? And what would we do if billionaire talk show host Oprah Winfrey had listened to everyone who ever said her weight would prevent her from having a successful career on television? There are endless stories of great people throughout history—from the Wright brothers to Martin Luther King, Jr.—who refused to accept other people's limiting beliefs about their dreams. Not only were they able to accomplish their goals, but they accomplished more than they ever imagined possible and helped millions of people in the process.

I have a patient who once told me he had "quit-itis." He never followed through on anything. "Can't" was a word he often used. This patient complained of an assortment of aches and pains and overall fatigue. One day he came into the office and said he was ready to quit being a quitter! Using The LifeLine Technique, we discovered the root cause of his self-destructive behavior and corrected the imbalances that were affecting how he felt about his own life. In addition, he made a commitment to follow The Five Basics for Optimal Health—quantity, quality and frequency of water, food, rest, exercise and owning his power. On his next visit, he reported a marked improvement in both his health and his attitude. Over the past year, he has faithfully maintained a healthy balance with The Five Basics and continues to strive toward optimal health. He has quit being a quitter.

"Try" is defined as an attempt to succeed. However, the subtext of the word is that we *expect* to fail. For example, you might say "I'll try to eat right," but you mean, "Sugar is very hard to resist." Or you say, "I'll try to go to the gym," but you mean "It's so hard to get out of bed in the morning." Or "I'll try to remember to take my supplements," when you actually mean, "I hate to take pills." The difference between trying and succeeding is staying in the present moment, making a *commitment* and using your *will* to *do your very best.* Your will is the driving force that allows you to expand your potential to succeed. Free will is the infinite amount of choices you have in any given situation and ultimately the choice you make based on what is right for you.

It is your lack of will, denial of free will, denial of self and denial of love that are the motivation behind your use of "my," "can't" and "try." This is not a judgment. What you are actually doing is embracing fear. When you deny your will in any situation—from the most magical experience to the most challenging, hurtful, depressing, spiteful, grieving situations imaginable—you are embracing fear.

During a recent service of Rosh Hashanah (Jewish New Year), our rabbi gave a wonderful sermon. He talked about a little boy who showed his teacher a picture of the earth. As an experiment, the teacher tore the picture into little pieces and instructed the boy to put it back together again. In a short amount of time, the child came back with the picture taped together.

"How'd you do it so fast?" the teacher asked.

"On the other side of the earth was the picture of one person," the child responded. "Putting that one person back together helped me put the earth back together."

In order to heal the earth you must first put yourself back together; you must heal your own life. The words "my," "can't" and "try" are representative of the state of imbalance and dis-ease in your subconscious mind. "My," "can't" and "try" are symptoms of the subconscious mind's perpetration against the body. Own your power by doing your best; unconditionally respect, honor and love yourself by choosing to take responsibility for the words you use. The impact of your choice will send a ripple outward to heal the earth, one person at a time.

CHAPTER SIX

The Journey of Your Spirit

The Journey of Your Spirit is to reconnect with the power of Infinite Love & Gratitude. Infinite means the universe, or the collective conscious, that has no beginning or end. Love is the universal power that propels life; it fuels your will and enables you to face and overcome challenges. Gratitude empowers you to go through life without judgment. With gratitude you see the value of any experience as an opportunity, rather than being a victim of your circumstances.

From Dr. Emoto's work and our objectifying The LifeLine Technique, we know that the intention, words and acts of "Infinite Love & Gratitude" transform the molecular structure of water; the same water that makes up our cells. This transformation enables the electromagnetic field of the body to flow freely. The electromagnetic field is the energy that nourishes the body, facilitating its ability to heal. When the electromagnetic field of the body is flowing freely, you will find that your ability to create your reality through your intention and achieve optimal health occurs effortlessly.

The law of conservation of energy and matter states that energy can be neither created nor destroyed; it just changes form. Because you are an energetic being, there is a part of you that is eternal—it was not born, nor will it ever die. Energy has polarity, a positive and negative charge that radiates an electromagnetic field. Your body's electromagnetic field is your spirit. Keep in mind that when I refer to spirit, I am not talking about religion. I am referring strictly to the electromagnetic field of the body.

Many people recognize this electromagnetic field as life force. In the Introduction, I discussed it briefly in relationship to Einstein's theory of relativity. When the body's electromagnetic field flows freely, the physical body detoxifies and heals on its own.

The electromagnetic field has what is called a superconscious. The superconscious is where the mind resides and where all emotions begin. Every experience is attracted into your life through the electromagnetic attraction or repulsion of the superconscious mind. These frequencies of energy travel through protein receptors within the senses and the skin and are then processed within the primordial centers of the brain.

In the 1950s, neurologist Paul MacLean, M.D., considered to be one of the world's greatest brain scientists, proposed that the skull held not one brain but three. He called it the "triune brain." Dr. MacLean, who is the former director of the National Institute of Mental Health's Laboratory of Brain Evolution and Behavior in Poolesville, Maryland, says the three brains operate like "three interconnected biological computers." His research has found that each has "its own special intelligence, its own subjectivity, its own sense of time and space and its own memory." These three brain centers are referred to as the neocortex, or neo-mammalian brain; the limbic system, or paleo-mammalian brain; and the brain stem and cerebellum, or the reptilian brain. Each of these three brains is connected by nerves to the other two, but each seemingly operates as its own brain system with distinct capacities.

It had previously been assumed that the highest level of the brain, the neocortex, dominated the other, lower levels. Dr. MacLean, however, has shown that this is not the case. His research has demonstrated that the physically lower limbic system, which rules emotions, can hijack the higher mental functions when it needs to.

The oldest brain, the reptilian brain, includes the brain stem and the cerebellum. In animals, such as reptiles, the brain stem and cerebellum dominate. In humans, the reptilian brain has the same type of archaic behavioral programs as snakes and lizards. It is rigid, obsessive, compulsive, ritualistic and paranoid. It is "filled with ancestral memories" and repeats the same behaviors over and over again, never learning from past mistakes. This brain controls muscles, balance and autonomic functions, such as breathing or the rate at which the heart beats. This part of the brain is always active, even during deep sleep. Examples of reptilian brain behaviors are road rage, checking your appearance in a mirror, long multiplication and putting together a jigsaw puzzle.

Dr. MacLean was the first to coin the name "limbic system" for the middle part of the brain. The limbic system is concerned with emotion, attention, affective (emotionally charged) memories, instincts, feeding, fighting, fleeing and sexual behavior. Everything in this emotional system is either "agreeable or disagreeable." Survival depends on avoidance of pain and repetition of pleasure. It helps to determine valence (whether we feel positive or negative toward something), salience (what gets our attention), unpredictability and creative behavior. According to Dr. MacLean, the limbic system is the seat of our value judgments, instead of the more advanced neocortex. It decides whether our higher brain has a "good" idea or not, whether it feels true and right.

The neocortex, also known as the superior brain, comprises almost the whole of the hemispheres. The higher, cognitive functions, which distinguish humans from animals, are in the neocortex. In humans, the neocortex takes up nearly two-thirds of the total brain mass. The neocortex is divided into left and right hemispheres, the famous left and right brain. The left half of the neocortex controls the right side of the body, and the right half controls the left side of the body. The right brain is more spatial, abstract, musical and artistic, while the left brain is more linear, rational and verbal.

The unification of the three brains enables the electrical frequency of our thoughts, feelings and beliefs to be integrated into behavior. The reptilian system will respond in a reflexive manner to an experience for survival purposes. Once processed through the reptilian brain, the limbic system will transform the electrical frequency of an experience into emotion and memory. When an experience is perceived as non-threatening, it will be sent to the neocortex for processing. If an experience is perceived as life-threatening or beyond the capacity to adapt or cope, the limbic system will inhibit the emotion from being processed by the neocortex.

Overwhelming feelings and painful experiences are downloaded and stored in the limbic brain. This takes place automatically and on a subconscious level in a single millisecond of time, capturing all of the sensory data, feelings and perceptions of the traumatic experience. Since the 1970s, through the work of famed hypnotherapist, Milton Erickson, we have known that trauma triggers a spontaneous state of self-hypnosis that binds us to the emotional pain of the traumatic event. In other words, overwhelming emotional experiences induce a natural, hypnotic state as a way of containing pain and fostering survival. These hypnotic states form the basis of disease and pain within the body, mind and spirit. This is the way the subconscious mind disconnects from emotions. It is that subconscious disconnection that inhibits the journey of your spirit.

Every thought, feeling and belief that you have originates from the collective conscious. Your electromagnetic field, or spirit, will attract specific frequencies of energy that will be filtered through your sensory receptors into your body. The limbic system transforms these thoughts, feelings and beliefs into emotion. Emotion is energy *in* motion. Its natural state, whether it is within the collective conscious or within your body, is to stay in motion. Ultimately, to enable your body to function optimally, emotions need to be felt and then expressed. Your emotions are the intermediate state between your mind and your body. They are associated with your limbic system, which integrates the neocortex and the reptilian brain. When you have a subconscious disconnection from an emotion lying dormant within the limbic brain, it will continue to maintain a separation between your conscious mind (neocortex) and the body (reptilian brain).

From my experience with The LifeLine Technique, I have come to the conclusion that the limbic system acts as a stopgap to prevent trauma or shocking experiences from being processed by the neocortex. Instead, the traumatic experience waits to be released. When the subconscious memory of the trauma is triggered by any one of the senses, a signal is sent from the limbic system directly to the reptilian brain center. The signal of the trauma is blocked from connecting to the neocortex due to the emotions in the subconscious mind. The body does not know the difference between reality or imagination. When the trauma is triggered the body will begin to respond as if it is experiencing the trauma for the first time. The body will not break the holding pattern of reacting in a survival-like fashion until the trauma is processed.

The reptilian brain can only function as the reptilian brain—it is only able to support the survival mechanisms of the body, such as the basic physiological functions of circulation, respiration, digestion and elimination. It also is involved in mating, territorial behavior, pecking order, defense, aggression and the emotions of anger and fear. Subconsciously, the reptilian brain keeps the body functioning and behaving in a maladaptive way, creating a holding pattern of imbalance between the mind and body. On a conscious level, the person never learns from previous experiences because the trauma locked in his or her limbic system will trigger the same response over and over again.

When the limbic system processes an experience, a signal is sent to the neocortex. The process occurs during sleep when the eyes are going through rapid eye movement (REM) cycles. It is when the REM patterns are inhibited that emotions stay locked in the subconscious aspects of the brain. This signal of information to the neocortex facilitates a short-term memory to be processed into long-term memory, which then enables the person to learn a lesson from the traumatic experience and consequently stay in present time consciousness.

Lena came to see me the day after having a mammogram. The test revealed two invasive masses in her left breast. On the day of her appointment with me, Lena was scheduled to have another mammogram and an ultrasound in order to determine the extent of the masses. When I placed my hand over Lena's right breast her indicator muscle stayed intact. When I placed my hand over her left breast, however, her indicator muscle immediately became weak. Lena was frightened by the response of the muscle test and wanted to know if that meant she had cancer.

"I don't know," I responded. "I don't diagnose cancer. However, your body is showing that you are leaking energy from your left breast." I ran The LifeLine Technique to the left breast until the weak indicator muscle tested strong.

While I was working with Lena, she said to me, "I knew I would get cancer." I asked her how she knew that and she replied, "I told my husband, 'If I don't divorce you, I'm going to get cancer.'"

I used The LifeLine Technique to release Lena's limiting belief that she would get cancer unless she divorced her husband. Afterwards, I used The LifeLine Technique to create positive attractor fields of health and well-being by having Lena make positive, declarative statements. The entire treatment took fifteen minutes. Lena left the office feeling lighter, stronger and empowered.

Six hours later, I received a call from Lena. Her doctor had taken six mammograms and two ultrasound tests of her left breast but he did not find any sign of the masses. These follow-up results astonished and confused him. He told Lena that the first test was probably misinterpreted. But Lena had seen the pictures. She told me she felt physically different following the treatment we did with The LifeLine Technique. She knew the masses went away as a result of the treatment.

The internalized emotion of "I know I'll get cancer if I don't divorce you" created a holding pattern between the limbic and reptilian brains, leading to a decreased flow of life force in Lena's left breast. With The LifeLine Technique, we released the stop-gap that was inhibiting Lena's limiting belief from being processed by her neocortex. Once removed, the healing occurred all on its own.

The authentic expression of your emotions creates the opportunity for you to find or stay on your true path. It is through feelings of pain or discomfort that you recognize you need to reconnect to your true path. When your emotions that have been internalized within the subconscious mind are triggered, the molecular structure of the water that makes up every one of your cells instantly begins to change and break down. This breakdown diminishes your body's ability to conduct energy. It is truly the health of the water in your body's cell composition that enables your electro-magnetic field, or spirit, to flow without resistance. "Infinite Love & Gratitude" enhances the molecular structure and beauty of your cells, thereby providing the perfect environment for health and well-being.

With The LifeLine Flow Chart and the power of Infinite Love & Gratitude, current challenges, past traumas and shocking experiences can be released from the subconscious centers of the limbic brain and processed by the neocortex in an instant. You will be able to face health issues, past trauma, relationship challenges and financial difficulties with a fresh view. What you choose to do from this point of view is your choice, or free will.

CHAPTER SEVEN

The Passion of Free Will

The concept of *free will* has been misunderstood and taken to mean doing whatever you please. But it is more complex than that. Free will is the choice you have to express your thoughts, feelings and beliefs. It means being authentic not only by living your truth, but also in how you treat others.

Lack of communication is widely regarded as the number one source of conflict in society—from familial relationships and marriages to international relationships between countries, religions and different races.

The key to fully expressing your free will is maintaining rapport. Maintaining rapport means listening, understanding, expressing empathy and extending compassion, while allowing another person to do the same. Even if you disagree with that person, respecting his or her free will directly impacts your ability to express yours.

Rapport permits the expression of free will on both sides, even when two parties do not see eye to eye. Compassion can be defined as *com,* meaning "with," and passion, meaning "to suffer." Compassion gives you the opportunity to suffer with a person, sharing his experience without judgment even though you may have a different perspective on how you would handle the situation.

So many times you have a thought that you do not share because you are afraid of being wrong, judged, inappropriate or censored. This is why rapport is so critical. It is unconditional acceptance of free will—your own and that of other people. Many people expend far too much energy in acts of resistance: fear versus love; hatred of people because of their race, gender, age, sexual orientation or religious beliefs; disbelief in things they do not understand. Establishing rapport, in and of itself, is a healing response. It enables you to live authentically while honoring someone else's right to do the same.

Everyone's journey is different. It is of the utmost importance to recognize and honor the emotions created from your own experiences. Recognizing and honoring your emotions opens a direct link to your subconscious mind. This awareness empowers you to make the appropriate choice when you feel comfortable or uncomfortable in any given situation.

The challenge is to express your emotions—even when it is difficult—so as not to create subconscious patterns that result in dysfunction and eventually symptoms in the body. If the emotions from which we have subconsciously disconnected are not released, a disease pattern is set into motion.

Consider that thoughts are your free will and that they create feelings. Feelings guide you in every moment, creating either an emotional (internal) or sensory (external) reaction. When you deny your free will (thoughts), you deny yourself the opportunity to react authentically in a moment. For example, when you touch a flame, the feeling/reaction is, "Wow, this is hot!" The emotion may be fear or anger that you touched the flame. At the same time, the sensory experience is to instantly move your hand away. The difficulty arises when you do not recognize your feelings. At this point, pain changes to suffering. You continue to keep your hand in the flame, screaming while your hand burns. That is the denial of your free will.

The trick is not to wait until your hand is in the flame to feel the fire. Once your hand is in the fire, it is too late. You have already burned it. Your hand is going to need to heal once you remove it from the flame. It is going to take some time. However, when you increase your sensitivity to Present Time Consciousness (PTC), you become aware of your feelings and are able to feel the flame when it is subtly warm. In this way, the flame becomes an asset. You are able to create a healthy boundary with the fire by being in tune with the feelings you are currently experiencing. All of a sudden, this potentially destructive inferno transforms into a beautiful and meaningful bonfire. The fire can be used as a meeting place for friends and family, to roast marshmallows, sing songs and create wonderful memories.

The healing of your will begins with the acceptance of what you have denied, internalized or disconnected from. Before you get to where you are going, you have to be okay with where you are. Even when it is uncomfortable, this is the starting point.

Take, for example, addiction or self-destructive behavior. The denial is that you are numbing yourself from feeling the true essence of an experience. The starting point for healing and reconnecting to your will is acknowledging that you are addicted or that your behavior is self-destructive.

Another example of denied free will is choosing to live as if you are a victim of your circumstances, e.g., poverty, race, gender, religion, education or state of health. You have become compliant in accepting whatever situation validates your limiting/negative beliefs. How many times have you heard people say, "I've always been overweight, and that's just the way it is," or "Women are always treated like second class citizens, and there is nothing I can do about it!"? You may not be able to choose your circumstances, but you can choose your *reaction* to them. That is your free will.

Every human being has a choice. My idea of a completely harmonious world is one where we are unencumbered in our expression of free will and where we do not impose that will on other people. Because there is truth from every angle, it is ultimately about love and gratitude—the unconditional acceptance and respect of free will—your own and that of others.

The same holds true when you have feelings about a person or concerns about your health. If there is an immediate feeling of comfort or discomfort, it is very important not to deny your feelings so that the potential pain does not evolve into suffering. For example, what happens when someone offers you what sounds like an amazing opportunity, but you get an uncomfortable feeling in your gut that contradicts what is being said? By expressing your emotions about the situation, you will prevent this internal conflict from creating an imbalance in your body or a struggle in your life.

According to the precepts of Chinese medicine, different emotions have specific vibratory frequencies that electrically travel through the acupuncture meridians. For example, the emotion of grief travels through the lung meridian. Emotions of anger flow through the liver meridian. Fear travels through the kidney meridian. Every emotion is associated with a specific acupuncture meridian. When we are living in a state of subconscious denial of our will, the body is thrown into a subtle level of imbalance that creates specific symptoms depending upon the acupuncture meridian that is being affected. The following chart is a list of each acupuncture meridian and its corresponding emotions based on Chinese medicine and Neuro-Emotional Technique developed by Dr. Scott Walker.

Five Elements Emotion Chart

ELEMENT FIRE
Organ / Meridian
Small Intestine - Heart
Thyroid - Adrenals
Prostate - Testicles
Ovaries - Uterus - Pituitary
EMOTIONS
Lost, Frightfully overjoyed, Muddled instability,
Non-thinking, Abandoned, Deserted, Absent mindedness, Insecurity, Vulnerable,
Profoundly deep unrequited love,
Inappropriate laughing, Lack of emotion,
Talkative, Rapid mannerisms and speech,
Muddled thinking, Emotional instability, Up and down, Paranoia, Can't figure it out,
Non-emotive, Depleted, Suppressed,
Sluggish memory, Vivid dreaming

ELEMENT EARTH
Organ / Meridian
Stomach - Spleen
Pancreas
EMOTIONS
Over Sympathetic
Low Self-Esteem
Disgust
Expanded Self-Importance
Obsession
Egotistic
Despair
Nervous
Stifled
Lives Through Others
Over Concern
Hopelessness
Lack of Control - over events
Worried distrust

ELEMENT WOOD
Organ / Meridian
Gall Bladder-Liver
EMOTIONS*
Resentment
Anger
Galled
Stubborn
Emotionally repressed
Indecisive
Irrationality
Frustration
Aggression
Depression

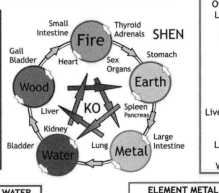

ELEMENT WATER
Organ / Meridian
Bladder - Kidney
EMOTIONS
Paralyzed Will
Fear
Miffed
Timid
Inefficient
Wishy-washy
Comme çi-comme ça
Dread
Bad memory

EMOTIONS © 1988
as researched by
Scott Walker, D.C. NET
www.netmindbody.com

ELEMENT METAL
Organ / Meridian
Large Intestine
Lung
EMOTIONS
Dogmatically Positioned
Grief
Crying
Compelled to Neatness
Defensive
Sadness
Yearning
Cloudy Thinking

Conscious and subconscious triggers constantly stimulate your emotions. Your will is the engine that propels your spirit along its journey. It is your spirit that feeds your body and makes it possible for it to adapt and heal. However, without an engine, or your will, your spirit is unable to move. Passion—the authentic expression of emotion—is the fuel for that engine. Your passion is what connects you to your purpose and enables you to use your intention to create abundance in your life. Embracing your life with passion is the key to acknowledging and honoring your emotions. Resistance occurs when you do not genuinely respond to your circumstances—when you attempt to control how life flows through you and how you flow through life.

I had a client whose blood pressure was 150/100. During a treatment, it became clear that she was attempting to control every aspect of her life. She recognized the connection between her need for control and the symptom of high blood pressure. By clearing out the subconscious emotions of fear and anger, her blood pressure went down to 124/84 within two days.

As life moves through you, make appropriate changes in the moment—express your emotions—so that you are not dragged down by life's undercurrent. Staying true to your purpose and embracing your life with passion helps you stay focused on achieving a desired outcome. Passion maximizes your ability to adapt to even the most unforeseen obstacles and actually uplifts your spirit so that you are able to create a new view with new possibilities.

High blood pressure has many causes. However, I believe the core reason so many people are taking blood pressure medications is that they fight rather than flow with life. They struggle with each experience creating resistance not only in their lives but in their bodies. In Chinese medicine it is said that blood follows chi. Chi is life force or the energy that moves us—emotion. It is when we attempt to control our emotions, rather than feel them and express them, that we increase the pressure in our lives, as well as in our cardiovascular system.

When there is increased resistance, there is decreased conductance, leading to the stagnation of your spirit. Stagnation results when you keep taking the same path, even though your emotions are telling you to go another route. Stagnation denies Present Time Consciousness (PTC), your authentic self, and is a manifestation of the denial of your will.

Owning your power and living true to your feelings facilitates the *chi* or life force that feeds and nourishes your body, which enables it to adapt and heal. The journey to awakening your spirit proceeds by expressing your free will, by living in PTC and by being open to the need and right of others to experience their own journey.

CHAPTER EIGHT

Symptoms: Gifts from Your Body

I was on a cruise with my wife, Sara. As we talked one morning, I began to think about how, as human beings, we have captured and filtered the earth's energy to create an easier way of life. For example, everything that happened on the cruise ship depended upon the harnessing of energy and the interdependence of all of its parts. The same relationship applies to the body. Applying The LifeLine Law of Transformation and Creation—*emotions transform energy; energy creates movement; movement is change; and change is the essence of life*—what happens to the body when your emotions are somehow stifled? What does the body do with *that* energy?

The subconscious is the storehouse of your experiences. When you stifle, stymie, ignore, deny or internalize your emotions, they get locked away. Because *emotions transform energy; energy creates movement; movement is change; and change is the essence of life*, they do not just sit in the storehouse waiting for permission to be released. They keep moving, banging up against the locked door, sending out below-the-radar messages to your physical body through the autonomic nervous system (ANS). When the physical body gets these messages, it searches for places to put them. It is when the emotions of the subconscious mind are triggered that the ANS begins to respond in a survival-type fashion. What is important to recognize is that subconscious means automatic. You are not able to rationalize the behavior of the subconscious mind. Its intention is aimed towards survival. However, the situation that is triggering the response does not warrant a survival response. The result of a prolonged subconscious response is complete and utter exhaustion of the body from the constant triggers of internalized emotions.

The longer your emotions remain disconnected, the greater the impact it has on the physical body, resulting in the body becoming imbalanced. The only time you are aware of your subconscious mind is when it uses a symptom to get your attention. Sometimes that symptom is so deep that it first appears as something as trivial as a headache or elbow pain. But unless you are in tune with your body, you may be missing what the subconscious mind is telling you; you may be missing the connection to how your body is *expressing* itself. Awakening to The LifeLine Technique helped me realize the subconscious connection between the body's imbalances—due to trapped, unexpressed emotions—and symptoms.

When you have a symptom, such as a headache, nausea or back pain, it is the body's way of creating dialogue. Symptoms are a language, just like French, Hebrew, Spanish or English. A symptom is really dis-ease, and dis-ease is the voice that the body uses to express imbalance. Imbalance is not the same as a breakdown; when the body is leaning in one direction or the other, that is an imbalance. For example, diarrhea, vomiting and fever are signs of imbalance—they are the body's innate intelligence triggering the need to purge poisonous substances. When you are able to bring the body back into balance, it prevents the dis-ease from becoming pathology (a diagnosable disease).

Symptoms are a gift. Pain is a gift. They are the body's way of saying that it is time to heal whatever emotions you have internalized, denied or disconnected from. With this in mind, when you are experiencing symptoms, instead of saying *"I'm getting sick,"* keep the dialogue going by stating, *"My body is beginning to heal."* Your body is actually providing you with an opportunity to listen. This attitude of gratitude enables the molecular structure of your cells to be in a healthier state, shortening the time it will take for your body to regain balance.

The five most dangerous words you can ever say to yourself are: "Maybe it will go away." When you are confronted with physical or emotional symptoms and choose merely to hope they will go away, rather than to determine why your body is communicating with you in this manner, you are putting your life at risk. You are missing the opportunity to engage in an internal dialogue of health on both a conscious and subconscious level. Unfortunately, we have been taught by our parents, teachers, medical doctors, and now by the pharmaceutical companies through television advertisements, to look at symptoms as the enemy. We have been taught that the body produces symptoms because it is at war with itself, and the secret weapons to deal with illness or disease are pharmaceutical drugs. But taking pharmaceutical drugs beyond the scope of emergencies could either worsen or actually silence the symptoms, inhibiting the body's innate ability to heal. As a consequence, the original imbalance is now prone to become a diagnosable disease, commonly referred to as pathology. Taking medications for every symptom stops the crucial dialogue between the body and the subconscious mind.

For example, as reported in major media throughout the United States in the spring of 2004, the USFDA's Center for Drug Evaluation and Research sent a letter to drug manufacturers requesting label changes on antidepressants warning of possible suicide, worsening depression, anxiety and panic attacks in adults and children. Ten of the most often prescribed antidepressants were on the list: Prozac (also sold generically as fluoxetine), Zoloft, Paxil, Luvox, Celexa, Lexapro, Wellbutrin, Effexor, Serzone and Remeron.

Does this mean that antidepressants are not necessary? No. However, the indiscriminate use of them is beyond frightening and needs to be regulated much more carefully. We are so conditioned to take a pill the moment we endure a painful, scary or challenging experience. The consequences are grave. It is time to take responsibility for being on medication. Begin by educating yourself about the meaning of symptoms and stress. Otherwise, we will continue to experience the devastating effects of overmedicating.

Depression is anger turned inward; anger at oneself. Depression leads to a molecular breakdown in the structure of the water that makes up our cells. This causes stagnation in our life force, which results in the body communicating with symptoms. Unless the emotion of depression is embraced as an opportunity to move through a challenging experience, it will continue infinitely until the experience is embraced.

For optimal health, it is imperative to allow the body to communicate rather than to suppress its symptoms. It is crucial for you to learn the language used by your body every moment of every day of your life. This book is an instruction manual in the most important language you will ever need to learn—Human Body Language!

I saw a new patient who came to see me one week after she was told she no longer had cancer. She was diagnosed with a grade four squamous cell carcinoma of the left tonsil that had metastasized to her lymph nodes. She underwent radical surgery to remove the tonsil and twenty-two lymph nodes in her neck. She also underwent eight weeks of chemotherapy while concurrently receiving twelve weeks of radiation. She stated that the treatments had left her without the ability to produce saliva, to taste or to swallow efficiently. She has a feeding tube directly connected to her stomach and a main line in her chest to administer medications. She takes morphine every evening to sleep and is on an experimental chemo pill that is supposedly going to prevent reoccurrence of the cancer. Her doctors recommended that she use a nutritional supplement that is loaded with sugar. She stated, "I feel like a train wreck."

During our first treatment session, I wanted to be sure her subconscious mind was not going to sabotage her goals of optimal health. She was congruent with her goals, so I began to focus on where her body was speaking the loudest. I found that her body was leaking energy from her neck and the left side of her face. The emotion of depression came up when I ran the LifeLine Flow Chart. Her body expressed a subconscious death wish that was associated with the depression. She told me that she had been feeling depressed ever since her husband left her and their three children seventeen years before. She had a limiting belief about loving herself unconditionally that inhibited her from releasing the depression. We discovered that the limiting belief originated when she was five years and seven months, when she was told that she had learning disabilities and that she could not do the things that "normal kids" could do. She bought into these limitations as if they were fact, and the depression that she internalized since the age of five years and seven months continued to devastate her mind and body to the point that it practically killed her.

When she left my office, she noticed that her neck and face felt lighter and full of life. She was empowered by the knowledge that she was not a victim of cancer, but rather her body was expressing the emotional pain she had subconsciously disconnected from for so long. She was ready to heal and begin to listen to the language her body so urgently wanted her to understand.

It is important to understand the concept of *emotion* on a much deeper level. Dr. Candace Pert, a noted neurobiologist and the author of the book *Molecules of Emotion,* has proven that neuropeptides—the chemicals triggered by emotions—are thoughts converted into matter. *Webster's New World College Dictionary* defines emotion as "complex reactions with *both mental and physical* manifestations." Dr. Pert's research discovered that emotions reside in the body and physically interact with cells and tissues.

As I said earlier, symptoms are a gift. Sometimes gifts have very strange wrapping paper, but once unwrapped they will turn into exactly what is needed at that moment. One of the unique and simple aspects of The LifeLine Technique is that it empowers you to use symptoms to access the *real* source of the imbalance—the subconscious mind—and release internalized, denied and disconnected emotions. Bringing those emotions to light and transforming them with the power of Infinite Love & Gratitude opens the body to healing. It is akin to unplugging a stopped up drain so that the water can flow freely through the pipes.

The following chart represents the cycle between optimal health and death:

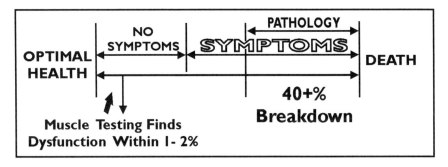

Pathology literally means a diagnosable disease. For pathology to be recognized in a blood test, urinalysis, MRI, mammogram or bone scan, the body must have already degenerated 40+ percent. The irony is that when a diagnostic test comes back "positive," it means you have a disease! This is the point at which most people recognize that their body is imbalanced because, prior to this, they were ignoring or covering up the subtle symptoms, e.g., cough, rash, allergies and headaches, with over-the-counter drugs.

What happens when you have symptoms but the test results are within the "normal" reference ranges? That is when doctors prescribe medications that scientifically have been proven to eradicate *symptoms*. But when you do not have a *diagnosable* disease, taking medication for the symptoms is like playing Russian roulette, often with fatal consequences. As reported in the July 26, 2000, issue of the *Journal of the American Medical Association* (*JAMA*), a study of hospitalized patients found that an estimated 250,000 people die each year from iatrogenic (induced by a physician's activity, manner or therapy) causes, making it the third leading cause of death in the United States, after heart disease! Figures from a Harvard medical practice study, reported in a 1996 *JAMA* article, also noted that widespread use of medication to relieve minor pain has caused a national epidemic. Nearly 20,000 people have died from bleeding stomach ulcers, and close to 200,000 people annually have been hospitalized as a result of using over-the-counter drugs to treat minor pain. I believe that these numbers are even far greater than what has been documented.

Whenever you take a pill for a symptom without looking for the underlying cause, you are telling the body, "Shut up, I don't want to hear you." By ignoring what your body is telling you, you are turning off your body's natural ability to heal, thus placing the body in a survival mode. This denial or silencing of the body's communication is what slowly but surely leads to pathology.

Your body will never heal in a survival mode. It is working too hard just to survive, just as if it is running away from a tiger. Your body does not need to worry about food digestion or boosting its immune system while outrunning a tiger.

The survival aspect of the nervous system means that your body is focusing on the task of staying alive. Your heart rate increases, respirations increase, and all of your blood rushes away from your internal organs, thus giving your body the instant energy it needs—in the form of oxygen, nutrients and blood glucose—to deal with a tiger. All of your muscles tighten so that you can react more quickly, either to fight or to turn 180 degrees and run away.

Your body is numb to any symptoms when you are in a survival mode. You are fooled into thinking nothing is wrong because you have been trained that not having symptoms is the same as being healthy. If you are always operating in a survival mode, i.e., under a lot of stress, you do not feel symptoms until it is too late. Have you ever known a person who worked ten to twelve hours a day and never missed a day of work? Often, three to six months after retiring, the person drops dead of a heart attack. This is such a common scenario because your body is simply unable to spin at the fastest RPMs for extended periods of time. It is only able to sprint efficiently for short periods. It will provide you with enough energy to dash away from a tiger. While it is overwhelmed by the immediate need to survive, your body cannot and will not heal.

When your body is running on overload or in survival mode, the energy boost it feels is more like the one you get from drinking coffee rather than from being well rested or from exercising. You *know* the difference. There are subtle feelings that the body creates in every experience. It is through these feelings that you will gain insight into when your body is numb and in a survival mode, or just feeling great. Recognizing the difference is one of the keys to living an optimally healthy life. That may be difficult because of the way in which many people live their lives—drinking coffee and diet sodas, eating fast food, and taking medication for every symptom. In effect, if you are numbing yourself with food, alcohol, drugs (prescribed and street), sex, shopping or work, you are creating patterns of self-destruction that lock symptoms into place. The symptoms have become a prison. Before you realize it, multiple dysfunctions on several different levels are expressing themselves as symptoms. Your body ends up compensating, moving symptoms around like chess pieces, and sometimes you are fooled into thinking that the *issue* or challenge is gone.

It is important to know *how* to listen to the body's *voice,* which speaks emotionally, biochemically, structurally and/or spiritually. This is where the responsibility falls into the hands of the individual. A thorough understanding of **The Five Basics for Optimal Health—quantity, quality and frequency of water, food, rest, exercise and owning your power**—will enhance the course your health will take.

Emotionally, the body's voice may speak with irritability, fear or insecurity. Limiting beliefs may trigger your biochemical body to speak with hormonal imbalances or low blood sugar. Structurally, the body may communicate with low back pain or muscle aches. Every symptom of the body is an expression of the body's innate intelligence. Be open to feel, and you will gain access to and understand the infinite ways in which the body is ready to heal.

Chiropractic Philosophy, by Dr. Joseph B. Strauss, outlines three common approaches used to understand the body's language: mechanistic, pseudo-mechanistic and vitalistic. The mechanistic approach seeks a silver bullet. Webster's Dictionary defines mechanistic as the "doctrine that natural processes are mechanically determined and capable of explanation by the laws of physics and chemistry." The true mechanist believes that only science is real; he rejects any vitalistic concept, anything that cannot be empirically demonstrated.

A pseudo-mechanistic individual acknowledges the existence of forces he cannot see or demonstrate. But in practice, he denies the ability of these forces to run the universe or his body. Most people fall into this category. They recognize that a power greater than themselves created their body, that two half-cells, in roughly nine months, make a human being. Then, for the next seventy years, they deny that power and allow a finite mind with a mechanistic philosophy the opportunity to run it. They are like individuals who get up every morning and ask God to watch over them before they leave the house, but then put a rabbit foot, crystal or some other meaningful symbol in their pocket for luck before they leave. There is an inconsistency to it.

Vitalism is defined as "the doctrine that the processes of life are not explicable by the laws of physics and chemistry alone and that life is in some part self-determining." In other words, life is more than just chemical actions and reactions. If we take apart a pocket watch and put it back together properly, it will work. However, if we disassemble a living human being and reassemble it, even putting all the parts back in the right place, it will never work again. There is an inexplicable factor that cannot be seen or created in a laboratory.

Dr. B.J. Palmer, the developer of Chiropractic, called this factor *innate intelligence*. As we said earlier, Chinese medicine refers to this as *chi*. Ayurvedic medicine refers to it as *prana*. In different religious texts it is referred to as the Divine, or Spirit. When we refer to spirit in this book, we are talking about the electromagnetic field, or the life force of the body.

The LifeLine Technique will help you to understand the vitalistic essence of symptoms and to facilitate the ability of your body's innate intelligence to heal. LifeLine Practitioners treat people, not disease. We focus on symptoms as the vehicle to understand the root nature of energetic imbalances. As you can see from the earlier graph, halfway between pathology and optimal health is the cutoff where symptoms begin to express themselves. Your goal should always be to strive toward optimal health and to be proactive by maintaining a healthy lifestyle.

CHAPTER NINE

Begin with Self-Love

Many people are victims of chronic pain, illness and premature death. They have been brainwashed by pharmaceutical companies to focus on eradicating symptoms, rather than taking responsibility for their health and getting to the root cause. As we now know, this view of eradicating symptoms will lead to further suffering. It is crucial that you actively participate in the conversation that your body is having with you at every moment.

Thoughts, feelings and beliefs are a by-product of your experiences. When you embrace life with Infinite Love & Gratitude, your body has a direct connection to the collective conscious, thus enabling it to do what it does best—heal. The human body as a mechanism has evolved to maintain balance and heal itself. It is when we disconnect from Infinite Love & Gratitude that the vitalistic essence of the body is inhibited, causing the body to break down and speak with symptoms.

The only time a pharmaceutical drug is necessary is in life-threatening situations. Otherwise, the human body is the best pharmacy on the planet. It is able to produce every chemical known and unknown to humankind. The only time that this pharmacy is not open for business is when we are disconnected. Infinite Love & Gratitude is the currency that keeps the body, mind and spirit in business.

You are your own best doctor. Rather than looking at symptoms as the cause, learn to use symptoms as a portal to discover why your body is talking to you in the first place. Every symptom in your body or challenge in your life is like a mosaic. When standing close to it, the mosaic's picture is blurry and has no meaning. However, when you stand back, you are able to appreciate how all the colors and pieces merge together to form a beautiful piece of art. Every thought, feeling and belief you have is a piece to your own personal art. Every color in the mosaic has meaning, as does every symptom or uncomfortable feeling with which your body speaks. The language your body uses to communicate with you is an opportunity for you to heal or create abundance in all areas of your life.

Whether you have emotional or physical symptoms, they are your body's way of saying, "I'm not happy with how you're treating me. You've gotten off track; it's time to focus on The Five Basics for Optimal Health.

Author Louise Hay, who popularized the connection between mind-body and healing, wrote in an essay in *The Handbook of the Heart*:

> *Many people contact me for help with health issues, even very serious ones. All I do is teach them to love themselves. They learn to look at what has gotten in the way of their love and health. . . . I have people look into a mirror, just look into their own eyes and say, "I love you."*

Healing begins when you love yourself unconditionally. Symptoms are an expression of your denial of the need for self-love. The first step of healing is to completely embrace who you are right now. When you neglect self-love, it is reflected in your relationships with others, in your health, in your work, and in every other aspect of your life. The LifeLine healing process helps you see how, when, where and why you have neglected your need for self-love. It helps you appreciate the journey that you have already traveled and prepares you for the road ahead.

I was in the middle of a treatment with a woman named Suzie. I noticed that she seemed distracted, and I asked her to get in touch with the conversation going on in her head.

"Right now, I'm feeling bad that you're running an hour behind and that there are several people sitting in the waiting room," she replied.

I asked her to focus on her feelings about the people who were waiting to see me. As she did that, Suzie began to recognize that she always put other people's needs and concerns ahead of her own. She started to cry when she realized that she *believed* no one would love her unless she put them first.

To heal, you must accept where you are and who you are, and love yourself unconditionally for being a perfect creation. Here are a couple of analogies: You have to deposit money in a bank before you withdraw it. When flight attendants give safety presentations before a plane takes off, what do they say about the oxygen mask? "Put on your own mask first so that you are able to help other people." Self-love is not self-indulgence, selfishness or self-centeredness. Self-love requires that you own who you are at this moment, without judgment. True happiness is discovered during the healing process; it is a by-product of the journey, not the end result.

Healing is about balance. By using the frequency of "Infinite Love & Gratitude," The LifeLine Technique balances the body so that it will be able to accept and harmonize the emotions you have subconsciously denied. Once balance is restored, the body's natural ability to heal itself is unleashed. Balance and therefore healing begins with self-love.

Chapter Ten

Healing the Real Pain

The body speaks the mind. It is very common for chronic health conditions to be triggered during stressful times. Asthma attacks, herpes outbreaks, low back pain and digestive disturbances all seem to be triggered when our lives are in turmoil. Symptoms become chronic when we are disconnected from our mind. They serve as a distraction to the *real* pain—the emotional pain in the subconscious mind. Emotional pain is experienced differently by everyone. We are subconsciously programmed by our families, society, race, education, religion or television to disconnect from our emotions.

Western medicine helps us to further disconnect by labeling us as if we *are* the diseases. Defining ourselves as a disease, such as an asthmatic or a diabetic, causes us to further numb the mind, perpetuating subconscious addictions. When I refer to addiction, I am talking about the *continuous*, subconscious internalization, denial or disconnection from a painful situation. Addiction is a symptom. We long to know our truth, but we are afraid. Our truth, according to author Marianne Williamson, is that "we are powerful beyond measure." We are afraid of our own power, so we subconsciously numb ourselves with chronic symptoms. Ask yourself this question: "Is there any aspect of my life that I am afraid to embrace without judgment?" If so, that makes you an addict.

While we are aware of addictions that occur on a conscious level, there are stronger addictions that occur on a subconscious level. We have all been subconsciously conditioned to disconnect, and that traps us in a cycle of addiction. Not only are we left numb *with* chronic pain and disease, we have bought into and *defined* ourselves in terms of those diseases.

We must first recognize that chronic disease processes are a way that the body numbs emotional pain within the subconscious mind. To heal the chronic process, we have to heal the emotional pain in the subconscious mind. Otherwise, at some time, some place, the subconscious mind will be triggered, recreating the pattern within the body and causing the chronic health condition to reappear. The body will respond to the trigger in a classical conditioning response, and the breakdown will begin again. Every symptom, including addiction, is an opportunity, a gift from the body, as well as a gift from the mind. Whether or not a symptom becomes chronic—a subconscious addiction—is determined by our ability to stay connected to an experience when facing emotional and physical pain.

I had a breakthrough with a long-term patient who had been diagnosed with Crohn's disease and kidney stones. Peter, who is forty-five, had already undergone multiple surgeries, resulting in the removal of several feet of his intestines. He acknowledged that he had not been taking good care of himself and realized that this self-destructive behavior had deeper roots. However, he was unaware of the source of his self-destructive behavior. Peter's body had been classically conditioned to numb itself on a subconscious level by creating inflammation in his bowel. Subconsciously, when he would have certain thoughts in his mind or feelings in his body, the inflammation in his bowel would be triggered.

To facilitate Peter's ability to heal, it was important to help him become aware of the subconscious patterns that first triggered the inflammation in his bowel. To begin The LifeLine treatment, I had Peter say, "I'm okay that I'm an addict." By making this declarative statement, Peter was able to release the subconscious holding patterns that were perpetuating chronic disease. Unless a subconscious addiction is acknowledged and made conscious, we remain unaware of the subconscious emotions that are manifesting as chronic disease.

The LifeLine Flow Chart led us through six layers into Peter's subconscious mind. Each layer had to do with Killer-Thought Viruses and Death Modes (explained in detail in Chapter 15) that were programming his body to form chronic illness. His life force had diminished in each of the Five Elements, depending upon the layer in which we were working.

At one point, a limiting belief appeared in his fourth (heart) chakra, having to do with his inability to unconditionally love himself. While running The LifeLine treatment on Peter, I discovered that the original occurrence of this limiting belief began at two hours and forty minutes of life. He told me that he was born six weeks premature, his umbilical cord was wrapped around his neck, and that his mother almost died while giving birth to him. At that moment of his birth, in a state of lowered resistance and vulnerability, his subconscious mind created a limiting belief that he did not love himself unconditionally and a Killer-Thought Virus of feeling hopeless, worried and low self-esteem.

Through this treatment, we discovered the inflammatory bowel disease that formed in his body later in his life was the result of this initial trauma. The inflammation in his bowel was used as a way for him to subconsciously disconnect from the extreme pain of his birth. Peter felt a major shift in his mind and body after the treatment. He said, "I feel like you've just helped me open my mind to a healthy state of being. I am now ready to heal."

Peter is now consciously aware of his responsibility for maintaining his health. He also knows that every time his bowels act up, not to blame it on the Crohn's disease, but rather to embrace the symptoms as a gift and to focus on The Five Basics for Optimal Health.

Owning your power and being authentic in the moment enables you to break the cycle of chronic disease and subconscious addiction. Acknowledging your experiences without judgment empowers you to accept who you are and where you are in life. Choose now to live a fearless life by embracing your truth with Infinite Love & Gratitude.

CHAPTER ELEVEN

Beliefs and Healing

Sara and I have three cats—Floyd, Zen and Buddha. Zen is the biggest of the three. He is fairly agile, even at twenty-three pounds. Every time we use our electric can opener to open the cats' food, Zen is usually the first one in the kitchen. A couple of years ago, I opened a can of food, but Zen did not come bounding into the kitchen. I went looking for him to make sure he got some food before his brother, Buddha, ate it all. I found Zen, picked him up and placed him on the floor. When I did, he fell on his face. I thought, "Oh my God, I dropped him! He broke his leg!" I quickly realized, however, that Zen did not have a broken leg; he was paralyzed.

I immediately began to perform acupuncture, energy work and chiropractic treatments on Zen, but I did not notice any improvement. The next day, I took him to a veterinarian. The vet conducted several tests, including a sensory test in which he squeezed Zen's paw with pliers. There was no reaction. He asked whether Zen had exhibited any signs of pain before the onset of the paralysis. I shook my head. The vet's diagnosis was that Zen either had a herniated disc or an embolism lodged in his cervical spine. I have been trained in veterinary manipulative orthopedics, and I am very in tune with the structural health of "my boys." I knew there was no way Zen had a herniated disc. However, I was not sure about the embolism.

Within a week, I took Zen to the vet again because I felt he still was not improving. I was heartbroken because I thought I was going to have to put Zen down. I did not want him to suffer any longer, and if he was going to die, I wanted to be holding him in my arms. However, when the vet conducted another sensory test by squeezing Zen's paw with pliers, Zen hissed. The vet said the sensation in Zen's paw showed that he was moving in the right direction.

Six days later, Zen was visibly making progress. A week after that he was walking and jumping up on chairs. The vet was as amazed as we were. Zen had achieved a complete, miraculous recovery from total paralysis. Eight more lives to go!

Zen's recovery helped me to realize that animals, like children, do not have limiting beliefs that impede their healing. They do not question the possibility that a treatment, even if it is non-conventional, can help them heal.

My understanding of the connection between beliefs and healing came from experiences with two patients. Molly, who was fifty-three, came to see me after her medical doctor said she had one month to live. She was diagnosed with stage four pancreatic cancer, which she had been told was fast-growing and terminal. She did not want to die with her head in the toilet because of chemotherapy; if she was going to die, she said, she wanted to die with her dignity and pride intact.

During our first session, I adjusted Molly's ribs, which enabled her to breathe more freely. When we began more intensive, holistic types of treatments, her body responded wonderfully. After an entire year of treatments, Molly decided to see her oncologist again, the person who had given her the "one month to live" diagnosis. She wanted to get a CT scan to see what was going on. The CT scan revealed that the cancer had not disappeared, but it had defied her doctor's prediction: the tumor had not grown. Despite that good news, Molly had hoped and expected that the cancer would have completely disappeared. At that moment, her belief that "everybody who has cancer must die" took hold. She died within six months.

My heart still aches with the thought of Molly's death. However, I am also filled with a strong sense of satisfaction and pride that as a result of our healing work together during those eighteen months, the "fast-growing," aggressive cancer had not grown at all. Molly was able to celebrate anniversaries, birthdays and have walks in the sun with her friends, pride and dignity intact. I grew so much as a physician and a person from my experience with Molly. I knew her prior to awakening to The Life-Line Technique, and I know that my experience with her was a huge stepping stone to its development.

Another patient, Bill, in his forties, was diagnosed with multiple sclerosis (MS) and was confined to a wheelchair when he first came to see me. After two to three months of treatment, Bill was walking laps around the office.

"Dr. D," he would say, "You're the Michael Jordan of doctors."

"It's not me, it's you," I would respond, laughing. "It's your body that is healing itself."

One day Bill did not show up for his appointment. I was surprised because he had never missed a session. I called and asked if he was all right.

"I just couldn't make it," he replied.

Bill never rescheduled. I never saw him again. I was still treating his wife, however, and I inquired why Bill no longer came to the office.

"He just doesn't *believe* in *this* anymore," she said.

"He was walking! What's going on?" I replied.

She simply shrugged her shoulders.

What *is* going on? *You are what you believe yourself to be.* Once you have created your *identity* based on limiting beliefs, it is difficult, even scary, to accept change. What is the source of beliefs? Your life experiences help to mold your beliefs, which are influenced by your relationships with your parents, siblings, spouses, partners, doctors, bosses, co-workers, religion, gender, race, age, the media, losses, traumas, and so on. With your senses—vision, smell, hearing, taste, touch and feelings—you are able to perceive the environment. From these life experiences, your *beliefs* are created.

It is through life experiences that you learn to identify with the value of a moment. Values give life meaning. They are the catalyst for choosing whether to transcend life's challenges or to be overwhelmed by them. When you value the infinite possibilities and potential of each moment, there are no limits to your beliefs.

Your perceptions of the outside world send signals to every cell in your body, telling it what is going on so that the body can adapt to its environment. Depending upon the situation, the body's nervous system will respond in one of two ways: in a sympathetic/fright, fight or flight survival mode, or in a parasympathetic/relaxation or healing mode.

Dr. Bruce Lipton, a cellular biologist and author of the book, *The Biology of Belief,* documented the connection between perception and health. Dr. Lipton set out to discover the brain of a cell. He began the process by studying deoxyribonucleic acid, more commonly known as DNA.

DNA was discovered in the early 1950s. This scientific advance was the result of the Nobel Prize-winning work of two scientists, Dr. James Watson and Dr. Francis Crick, based on the initial research done by Dr. Rosalind Franklin. Since the discovery of DNA, technology and science have discovered many ways for using it—from genetic fingerprinting to identifying criminals.

At the heart of the scientists' work was the belief that DNA is the *brain* of a cell. That being said, if a person has the chromosomal, genetic makeup for breast cancer, inflammatory bowel disease or bipolar disorder, the belief was that he or she would eventually develop that disease. As a consequence, in this day and age, some women are having complete, bilateral, radical mastectomies without any physical sign of cancer due to a genetic evaluation of their DNA. The tragedy, as Dr. Lipton's research documented, is that DNA is *not* the brain of the cell.

Dr. Lipton conducted tests in which he removed the nucleus of a cell containing the DNA. He hypothesized that if DNA were the brain of a cell, something very predictable would happen when it was removed—the cell would die instantly, just as a person would die if their brain were removed.

Just the opposite occurred. The cell lived. Dr. Lipton discovered that the brain of a cell is its protein receptors, very thin membranes that function like a cell phone antenna, sending messages directly to the nucleus. These protein receptors are not only on the outside of a cell and the nucleus, but also in our senses, i.e., the rods and cones in our eyes, the cilia (hairs) in our nose and ears. All of our sensory receptors are made of protein, and protein, in an antenna-type fashion, picks up the vibratory frequencies of sound and light and sends the signal to our brain. The brain then sends a signal down the spinal cord to specific areas of the body, depending upon the message. When the protein receptors on the outside of individual cells receive the information, they send a signal to the nucleus where the messages are encoded. From that encoding, the protein *creates* the DNA for a specific cell so that the cell will adapt to its environment. The nucleus, according to Dr. Lipton's research, is in fact the reproductive system of a cell—it is the center of a cell's ability to regenerate.

Dr. Lipton's exhaustive studies also sought to discover how a cell responds to stimuli, similar to the way the brain reacts to the senses. He wanted to know how the liver, lungs or intestines respond to what is going on in the external environment. What he discovered, as explained in his book, is the link between beliefs and the state of health:

> *Cellular biologists now recognize that the environment (external universe and internal physiology), and more importantly our **perception** of the environment, directly controls the activity of our genes.*

At this very moment, your liver does not know you are reading this book; your lungs do not know what color shirt you are wearing; your intestines are not aware of the temperature outside. All of your organs rely on your senses to receive external stimulation so that your internal body will adapt optimally. Your autonomic nervous system (ANS) functions in a sympathetic/fright, fight or flight survival mode, or parasympathetic/healing mode. Dr. Lipton discovered a Catch 22: belief systems serve as a filter through which we perceive the environment.

Let me give an example. Suppose you are standing at a bus stop when a red Jeep drives by. The last time you were standing at a bus stop and saw a red Jeep, there was an accident. You had to leap out of the way to keep from being injured. On a sub-conscious level, seeing a red Jeep now triggers the limiting beliefs associated with the accident; it changes your perception of the situation and you feel you are in danger. That sense of danger sends a signal inside your body, to every organ, every muscle and every cell. You feel the need to run because of the *subconsciously perceived* danger. The sympathetic nervous system kicks in and the body goes into a survival mode. Inside your cells, the DNA is reproduced and continues to perpetuate patterns of fear, even though the red Jeep you see is not a present danger whatsoever.

Your limiting beliefs filter this benign situation and keep the trauma alive, causing your body to be more susceptible to breakdown. The survival mode is good for one thing, survival. Any extended state of survival beyond its inherent function leads to breakdown. A deer, for example, senses and hears a mountain lion before it actually sees it, based on its inherent survival skills. If the deer constantly walked around in fear of the mountain lion, it would lose its ability to truly recognize danger, thus creating a bigger threat than the lion.

Near the Arctic Circle, people's perception of their icy environment facilitates the creation of DNA that helps them adapt. Similarly, people who live along the equator have their own perception of their environment and their DNA has changed over the generations to allow them to adapt optimally.

Since September 11, 2001, we have all changed our perception about the possibility of planes crashing into high-rise buildings. That belief is imbedded in our protein receptors sending messages to cells throughout the body, creating DNA that causes many people to live in a fright, fight or flight survival mode every time they see an airplane. Consequently, with the occurrence of trauma, any experience similar to their collective social experience on a subconscious level will recreate the limiting belief locked in by the initial trauma. This experience results in the autonomic nervous system functioning in a survival mode. Suddenly, life becomes overwhelming and they are stricken with panic attacks, phobias and anxiety. The fear mechanism is lost and they are stuck in a holding pattern of disconnection and disease. The challenge is that they are unaware of the origin of the panic and anxiety, and its connection to the initial trauma.

There are certain belief systems that are anchored in our being. Holocaust survivors, Native Americans and descendants of slaves have their traumatic experiences imprinted in their protein receptors, which in turn are passed along through generations, creating certain perceptions and inherent belief systems.

The body responds to anything remotely similar to that trauma by increasing the production of protein receptors that are keeping the trauma alive. As a result, we continue to attract more experiences that facilitate the subconscious disconnection. For example, feelings of low self-worth, insecurity and shame will continue infinitely in a loop of complete annihilation until they are embraced by the conscious mind. Subconsciously we continue to attract relationships, jobs and other life experiences that trigger these emotions. This may seem self-destructive; however, through our feelings of low self-worth, insecurity and shame we awaken to the patterns and emotions lying dormant within us. By recognizing the symptoms of our body or the stress in our life as the language of the subconscious mind, we are able to break the subconscious addictions to pain and suffering.

In the film *What the Bleep Do We Know?* Dr. Joe Dispenza says:

> *If I change my mind, will I change my choices? If I change my choices, will my life change? Why can't I change? What am I addicted to? What will I lose that I am chemically attached to? And what person, place, thing, time or event that I'm chemically attached to, that I don't want to lose because I may have to experience the chemical withdrawal from that? Hence the human drama.*

Because 98 percent of our reality is subconscious and 2 percent is conscious, at the sensory level, we *miss* 98 percent of what is happening around us. Right now, without *consciously* thinking about it, do you know what your feet feel like touching the floor? Are you presently thinking of your mother's maiden name or her birthday? Are you aware of the emotions you are experiencing in this very moment? The subconscious mind is aware of this and much more.

The conscious and subconscious minds are portals that connect us to the physical body as well as to the collective conscious. The collective conscious is Infinite Love & Gratitude; it is the energy of the universe, which has been described as God by many religions. Think of the conscious mind as the tip of the iceberg and the subconscious mind as what lies below the surface. Each time we view the pain and challenges of life as an opportunity to heal, we take one step closer to being connected to our subconscious mind.

Emotions are our superconscious mind. The superconscious acts as an attractor field and is a combination of both the conscious and subconscious minds. When a subconscious emotion is triggered, an imbalance is created within the body. This imbalance affects the flow of our life force through our acupuncture meridians, resulting in the body expressing itself with physical symptoms and life expressing itself with emotional challenges. The type of symptom or challenge experienced is directly related to the acupuncture meridian that is not flowing freely.

These physical symptoms and emotional challenges are not a form of victimization, but rather they are an intricate language that our body and life are using to warn us, "Stay in the moment, no matter how challenging it may be, so that you can learn from the challenge and reconnect to your infinite potential." In fact, no matter how challenging or painful your emotions are, have faith, and embrace them with courage and passion. When you do, you will find that you are able to face any obstacle, achieve any goal, and overcome any trauma.

With the power of Infinite Love & Gratitude, The LifeLine Technique removes the roadblocks from the subconscious mind, creating a more conscious life. By opening the subconscious mind, the roadblocks to healing become more apparent, allowing us to view the potential dangers that exist more clearly. As with anything, the more one practices opening the subconscious mind, the easier it becomes to master and live life truly in the present moment.

At a recent seminar in Chicago, a woman was treated using The LifeLine Technique to help her release the limiting beliefs that were preventing her from losing weight. She first made a declarative statement about being okay with her present weight, acknowledging her current weight challenge. She was previously unaware of the subconscious holding patterns that were keeping her from losing weight. After harmonizing the internalized, denied and disconnected emotions about her current weight, she then made positive statements about the goals she wanted to achieve. We harmonized those subconscious patterns and within the next two weeks, she lost ten pounds. Coupled with The Five Basics for Optimal Health of proper quantity, quality and frequency of water, food, rest, exercise and owning her power, she had all the tools necessary to accomplish her goal. Amazing as it sounds, it is truly this simple. The first step is to reconnect to the subconscious mind.

Dr. Victor Frank, developer of Total Body Modification (TBM) always says: "If you keep doing what you've always done, you'll keep getting what you've always gotten." Our beliefs can do us harm, even if we are not aware of them. The most important thing is to recognize that we have the power to change. The first step is recognition. The second is speaking our truth: *I want health. I deserve to be financially secure. I am worthy of an authentic, reciprocal relationship. I will achieve my optimal body weight. I will live my life with passion. I will follow my true path in life.* Be open to the fact that the moment you decide your life will change, you have the power to transform the impossible into the possible.

By becoming aware of the fear-based beliefs that filter your sensory perception, you awaken the power to create positive, love-based beliefs that facilitate and attract what you desire. As with the woman who attended the Chicago seminar, harmonizing her limiting beliefs transformed her energy and created movement in her life that enabled her to lose the weight she desired.

Emotions transform energy, and energy creates movement. The movement that is in your life will determine the direction in which you are headed. The subconscious patterns that may be holding you back from achieving your dreams can now be harmonized with Infinite Love & Gratitude.

CHAPTER TWELVE

Freeing Yourself to Heal

There are two laws by which we live. One is the law created by man. This law provides society with guidelines for structure, safety and harmony. The other is created from the universe and is the law of nature. This law, when followed, reveals the path for us to find structure, safety and harmony within ourselves. When we break the laws of man, we are given a fine, a ticket or we are sent to jail. We are punished for not maintaining the structure, safety and harmony within our community. When we break the laws of nature, our bodies begin to break down. Symptoms are a sign that we have broken the laws of nature—we have disconnected from our emotions— and that we are not maintaining structure, safety and harmony within ourselves. The body only speaks with symptoms. Physically, we begin to have symptoms of pain, discomfort and dysfunction. Emotionally, we are stricken with depression, anxiety and fear. The police and judicial system uphold the laws of man. We ourselves are responsible for upholding the laws of nature.

We know that there are consequences for breaking the laws of man. However, we are not always conscious of the consequences for breaking the laws of nature. As is said, we are all spiritual beings having a human being experience. When we break the laws of nature, our human experience is disease. A tree whose roots are not planted firmly in the ground will not survive. A tree fed too much or too little water will not survive. All of the laws of nature that affect a tree also influence our well-being. Just as the tree has a natural rhythm that flows from season to season, so do we. Learning the laws of nature is essential for living optimally. Those laws include providing the body with the proper quantity, quality and frequency of water, food, rest, exercise and owning your power—being willing to change.

Diana, in her late thirties, came to see me because she was suffering with environmental illness. She was allergic to seemingly everything. Her situation was very challenging; I knew she had the potential to heal, and there was a part of her that knew it, too. However, she had a powerful fear—the fear of being well and of owning her power. When I encouraged her by talking about her body's ability to heal itself and her power to choose health, she accused me of being arrogant. Everything with which I encouraged her was met with a negative/limiting response.

"I can't heal," she said. "Everything makes me sick. You don't know what you're talking about." She had spent the last fourteen years "trying to get well," she said, and she believed I did not really understand what was going on with her. Diana never scheduled another appointment.

In her book, *Why People Don't Heal and How They Can,* Dr. Caroline Myss says:

I believe that we are all born with a certain packet of perceptions, of "that which we know to be true." One of the perceptions in the packet is that if we let go of certain things, our lives are going to change. And the reality is that we are actually more afraid of change than we are of death.

Dr. Myss refers to this belief as *woundology,* a kind of "welfare state of the soul" in which we prefer to remain caught in the pain of chronic illness, disease, addiction, past traumas and/or tragedies rather than to do the work needed to heal ourselves.

What is the source of woundology? I believe it is both fear of healing and lack of love, particularly self-love. For most of us, the fear of healing stems from our fear of change. Even if our current state is uncomfortable, it is at least *familiar.* Think about people who have been diagnosed with diabetes but who continue to maintain the same unhealthy lifestyles. Or what about people who stay in abusive relationships? Fear of change keeps us driving down the same streets to work every day. These behaviors are familiar on a primordial, core level. They are at the core of our subconscious mind.

As we attempt to move towards healing on a conscious level, the conscious mind brings in all of the data of its experiences; it becomes aware of possibilities. But those feelings are immediately met by limiting beliefs of pessimism, triggering self-doubt. Your subconscious mind sounds an alarm: if you change, you are not going to be loved. The radar flashes: *Beware. Change is unknown and painful.*

Hal and Sidra Stone wrote two books, *Embracing Our Selves* and *Embracing Each Other* that address this issue. The Stones believe that the human being is comprised of multiple energies. The primary energy inside all of us, they write, is a vulnerable child (inner child). Before a baby is born, his data is raw. He is a liquid computer ready to be programmed. During his gestation period, he takes on the emotions of his mother. After his birth, every touch, every noise, every movement, every experience programs that baby, influences who he will become and creates bonding patterns between him and his family. Those patterns will either stimulate or inhibit the flow of his growth.

How do you think we are affected by parents who are constantly critical or who use anger to express themselves? We would likely internalize our feelings, developing a response that is not an authentic expression of what our authentic needs really are.

Disease and health are both learned behaviors. We are born with the ability to express our basic needs. When we are hungry and need to be fed, we cry. When we want to be held and comforted, we kick and scream. When we are tired and need to rest, we become irritable and fussy. This expression of our basic needs is, on a core level, our expressing the need for love.

Love is the primary nutrient, both expressed and received, that feeds us and enables us to grow and adapt. When we are denied that love, we search for alternative ways to receive it. We have learned that certain behaviors are rewarded with love and turn to those to maintain the loving connection to our primary relationships. This denial of our authentic needs creates a scenario of self-destructive patterns, of not being able to own our power. We end up disliking the parts of ourselves we have denied and even, at times, hating those parts. That dislike or hate (both consciously and subconsciously) causes the molecular structure of the water that comprises our bodies to stagnate and become distorted. More critically, because water conducts electricity, our life force is inhibited, increasing our potential for breakdown and decreasing our potential for adaptation and survival.

At the very root of all desire is the desire to be loved. When messages from the environment tell you that being yourself could result in *losing* love, who do you become?

Because we want to be loved, we act in a manner that assures we will get approval. If the vulnerable child feels like singing and being playful, but the critical parent wants us to be quiet, we will be quiet. We disavow the part of ourselves that needs to laugh and sing. The singing, playful inner child becomes buried and disowned and retreats to the shadow side, a side that is scary to express. On the outside, we are very serious. But that is not our authentic self. For example, people born in Israel are called Sabras. They are named after a fruit that grows from a cactus. On the outside of a sabra are prickly thorns that protect it from being eaten. On the inside is a sweet delicate core. Israeli Sabras live in an environment where there is a constant threat of danger. Because of this, they are known for their tough countenance, while at the same time, their core is rich with tradition, insight and love.

Our vulnerable child is the intermediary between our primary self and our disowned self. Because the vulnerable child always strives to be loved, we create primary selves that assure love will remain. We disown our authentic self in order to maintain a loving connection with primary relationships, such as our parents.

What is the foremost reason, then, that so many people are afraid of getting well? The answer is the fear of losing love the moment we reclaim our disowned selves. There is a subconscious reaction, reminding us of the moment we denied our authentic self.

I am reminded of a quote that is most often attributed to the former president of South Africa, Nelson Mandela. It was actually written by author Marianne Williamson, and it appears in her book, _A Return to Love: Reflections on the Principles of a Course in Miracles_:

> _Our deepest fear is not that we are inadequate. Our deepest fear is that we are powerful beyond measure. It is our light, not our darkness that frightens us. We ask ourselves: "Who am I to be brilliant, gorgeous, talented and fabulous?" Actually, who are you not to be? You are a child of God. Your playing small does not serve the world. There is nothing enlightened about shrinking so that other people won't feel insecure around you. We were born to make manifest the glory of God that is within us. It is not just in some of us; it is in everyone. And as we let our own light shine, we unconsciously give other people permission to do the same. As we are liberated from our own fear, our presence automatically liberates others._

Fear of our own power causes us to maintain dysfunctional connections, no matter what the consequences. We have been brainwashed to believe that darkness (i.e., symptoms and challenges) is the root cause of our discontent. The truth is the source of darkness is denying our light. Owning our power and embracing love unconditionally releases the suffocating hold of fear. Symptoms and challenges are the lighthouse in the darkness that guides us to unconditional self-love. Just as Marianne Williamson so eloquently wrote, ". . . as we let our own light shine, we unconsciously give other people permission to do the same. As we are liberated from our own fear, our presence automatically liberates others."

Every aspect of life has the potential to create challenges for us stemming from the original incident when we denied a part of ourselves to maintain a love connection. It may feel far removed, but this is how we learn disease. When we view the symptoms related to relationship issues, health challenges, financial struggles and spiritual stagnation as an opportunity to free ourselves, we are free to create the life we desire; the life we are capable of living. In the meantime, the personas we have developed are an opportunity to find our Holy Grail, our connection to the Divine. Each and every persona provides a journey inward to discover our authentic self.

CHAPTER THIRTEEN

Your Personas and Healing

Webster's Dictionary defines "persona" as the "outer personality or fa-çade presented to others." Everyone has multiple personas. Depending upon the circumstances—whether you are with your parents, siblings, friends, co-workers, family, boss, strangers, or alone in a car listening to your favorite song—a different persona emerges. Sometimes your personas become compartmentalized or dis-owned, depending upon the circumstances.

David's father, Steve, constantly expressed anger. Steve was a walking time bomb ready to explode at any moment. Whenever David made a mess in the kitchen or his room, his father yelled and spanked him. If he received a grade less than a "B," Steve reacted with judgment and severely punished him. David learned how to tiptoe around his father by becoming overly tidy and making sure that he always received high grades in school. David subconsciously became aware of the subtle cues from his father and was able to sense Steve's anger by the tone of his voice and his body language. David lived in constant fear of being yelled at, judged and spanked. In re-sponse to his fear, he embraced the persona of a "pleaser" while denying his own in-dependent needs and desires. He learned how to maintain a superficially peaceful environment with his angry, volatile father. David disowned the child within himself that enjoyed living in the moment and acting upon his free will.

On a subconscious level, he dislikes the part of himself that yearns to make his father happy. The moment David denied his own needs, a persona was developed and a dysfunctional pattern was set into motion, affecting both his nervous system and acupuncture meridians. This pattern inhibited his ability to adapt to various situations when his free will was challenged. Because of David's denial, his body began to "talk" to him with migraine headaches and hypoglycemia. His doctor gave him several medications, but none of them helped with the symptoms.

Ultimately, the symptoms of chronic migraine headaches and hypoglycemia provided David with an opportunity to own his power by acknowledging and honoring what he had originally denied. With the power of Infinite Love & Gratitude we harmonized David's internalized emotions of anger, fear and grief. He no longer has migraine headaches and his blood sugar is stable.

If you have a health challenge that is not going away with basic treatments, the pattern of dysfunction in your body is likely being held in a different persona. Dysfunctional patterns are created when you respond to an experience out of fear rather than faith. Unless the persona with the dysfunctional pattern is specifically accessed, it will be extremely difficult to get to the core of the symptom.

Through The LifeLine Technique, you will be able to identify the number of personas a person has and to determine which ones hold dysfunctional patterns. If the persona being worked on is not the one that holds the dysfunctional patterns, then the dysfunctional patterns of imbalance will never be reached.

When you are reacting or acting out of a persona that has dysfunctional patterns, your electromagnetic field is not unified. This can be recognized as limiting patterns that continue to repeat themselves. Relationship issues, health challenges, financial struggles and lacking passion for life all stem from a non-unified electromagnetic field. When fear is your modus operandi, you hold on to old history to maintain the illusion of safety because it is familiar.

When your field is unified with Infinite Love & Gratitude, you will find it easy to accept your denials and tap into the infinite possibilities of the present moment. By unifying the electromagnetic field, the subconscious denials become conscious, enabling you to own your power and transform the dysfunctional patterns. Once the dysfunctional patterns are balanced, you will be able to embrace your experiences with faith and courageously live your life with intention and purpose.

With muscle testing, we discover at what age a dysfunctional pattern began and what occurred to cause a specific persona to develop. By harmonizing this persona, we get to the original source of the imbalance in the body-mind-spirit.

The experiences you are having now are the result of the light reflected from your past, just as the light we receive from the sun and stars comes to us from thousands of light years away. Once your electromagnetic field is unified, you will continue to experience situations that have been attracted to you from your past. However, there is a transition period before you begin to receive the light you reflect as a unified field.

Take a moment right now and *feel*. Scan your entire body with your mind. Begin at your head and take notice of your feelings of comfort and discomfort. When you discover an area that is holding discomfort stop and appreciate it. Pay attention to the depth or the intensity of the discomfort. Is it sharp or dull? Is it localized or diffuse? Is it deep or more superficial? Breathe deeply into your abdomen while you continue to appreciate the discomfort. Send Infinite Love & Gratitude to that area and pay attention to what happens to the quality of that feeling. You will begin to notice that it dissipates as you breathe. Now, move onto your neck, shoulders, arms, hands, chest and abdomen, scanning each area of your body. Stop when you come to an area that is holding tightness, heaviness, numbness or pain. Breathe and pay attention to whatever thoughts or images begin to flow in your mind. You may notice that a voice begins to speak inside of your head when you get to a particular area of discomfort. Embrace the thoughts, images, memories and voices and breathe as you send them Infinite Love & Gratitude. You are learning how to listen to the conversation that your body is speaking to you in every moment. Listening is the most important aspect of communication and will enable you to focus your intention to your body's authentic needs.

Many of us are engaged in a monologue when it comes to having a conversation with our body. It is a monologue of hate, judgment and criticism of the parts of ourselves that we want to disown. When our body speaks to us with symptoms and challenges, we either ignore the messages or tell our body to "shut up" by using medication or addiction. However, a healthy relationship requires a dialogue. The parts of ourselves that we hate, judge and criticize must be embraced with Infinite Love & Gratitude.

Learning to listen is the first step to having a dialogue. Whether it is a pain in a muscle, bone or region, it is our body's direct way of communicating. By paying attention to our feelings, we open ourselves to the poetic expression of our body's needs. Healthy communication provides a forum for authentic expression and listening without judgment. When we dialogue with our body in this manner, we will soon recognize our inner beauty, the flow of life and the infinite possibilities of being.

Dialoging with your body can be used in every experience you have in your life. Pay close attention to your feelings while talking to a friend, spouse or eating a meal. Embrace *all* of your experiences and *feel*. Notice the difference between comfort and discomfort that you are having in every moment. Then own your power, creating healthy boundaries and relationships along the way.

CHAPTER FOURTEEN

It's *Your* Responsibility

Some people have experienced the most horrific or inhumane circumstances and yet have found a way to persevere. The late Dr. Viktor Frankl was a Holocaust survivor, psychiatrist and author of *Man's Search for Meaning*. Curious as to why some people survived under horrendous circumstances and others did not, he discovered that people with passion for life, a deep spiritual conviction and optimism were survivors. He wrote: "Ultimately, man should not ask what the meaning of his life is, but rather must recognize that it is *he* who is asked. In a word, each man is questioned by life; and he can only answer to life by *answering for* his own life; to life he can only respond by being responsible."

As a result of his studies, Dr. Frankl developed an entire school of psychotherapy, which is known as logo therapy. He helped his patients overcome their horrific circumstances by working with them to regain their passion for life, deepen their spiritual beliefs, and become aware of emerging opportunities by taking full responsibility for their lives.

I have a patient named Chris who was diagnosed with ulcerative colitis, which allopathic physicians state is an incurable inflammatory bowel disease. He first came to see me after having been hospitalized. His situation was so critical he almost died. After taking Chris's history, I realized he was severely dehydrated and his blood sugar metabolism was severely imbalanced. It was also clear to me that it was difficult for Chris to express his emotions. He was having challenges in his family and did not know how to confront them. All of these situations contributed to the inflammatory process that was devastating his colon.

After his first treatment, Chris began to embrace The Five Basics for Optimal Health. He began by daily drinking one quart of water for every fifty pounds of body weight; adopting a healthy eating program and making time to sleep so his body would be able to heal. He gradually added an exercise regime as well as began to confront the stressful situations in his life by authentically expressing his emotions.

Chris took full responsibility for his health and always kept an optimistic attitude, even in the most difficult moments. Although Chris's allopathic doctor said he would have this condition for the rest of his life and that he would permanently be dependent upon medication, he has been healed from ulcerative colitis for two years and is no longer taking medication. Chris has made the commitment to maintain healthy lifestyles and now sees me for maintenance health visits.

In many ways, Chris's healing journey can be likened to a gauntlet, a notably difficult challenge. Many before him took up the gauntlet and won, surviving every possible situation imaginable. But when you have the attitude, "I'll never make it through," or you view yourself as a victim of your circumstances, you have given up without taking the first step.

Confucius said: *The journey of 1,000 miles begins with the first step.* The first step to healing is to take responsibility for your life. Even if you feel as if you do not have the tools to heal (money, access to healing professionals, parents, friends, religious groups and support groups), you have the innate capacity and the power to choose to heal. Begin with an optimistic attitude and trust that however long the journey takes, you can and will make it through. There is no right or wrong in terms of the amount of time it will take. Trust yourself to have experiences, even if they are scary. How do you trust yourself? There is a part of you, on some rudimentary level, that can tell when something is right or wrong. Go by what you are *feeling*. You just have to trust your instincts. Of the infinite number of roads you can take, the right one is the one you are on. Just keep going and do not ever give up.

When I was twelve, my dad gave me a plaque. It read: "Opportunity is often missed because it is disguised as hard work." Healing is hard work. It is focus, commitment and action. It is about the attitude you choose to maintain during difficult situations. How you choose to view a situation—either as an opportunity for change or as a victim—determines the outcome. Whether you heal, how you heal, when you heal—your beliefs, attitude and passion determine whether you are ready to take full responsibility and embrace the changes your life needs for optimal health.

CHAPTER FIFTEEN

Your Body's Emotional Expression

Every emotion travels throughout the body via the acupuncture meridians. When your emotions are not expressed, there is a decrease flow of life force that results in symptoms. As mentioned earlier, symptoms are a gift, the language your body uses to get your attention. By listening to your body, you awaken to the subconscious emotions that you have disconnected from, and you are able to respond to your body's needs.

Within the body, symptoms occur on three levels—emotionally, structurally or biochemically. The next three chapters will explain *why* there has been a decrease flow of life force in the body so that you can develop a comprehensive understanding of the body's language.

There are five ways in which the body expresses itself emotionally: **Thought Virus, Emotional Cancer, Personal Invasion, Shock** and **Life/Death**. Let me explain in detail how each of these manifest in the body.

I first read about **Thought Viruses** in the book, *Thought Viruses: Powerful Ways to Change Your Thought Patterns and Get What You Want in Life*, by Donald Lofland, Ph.D., a Neuro-Linguistic Programming expert. Dr. Lofland wrote about four different types of thought viruses: Trigger, Limiting, Killer, and Gemini Thought Viruses.

A Thought Virus is no different than the virus that causes influenza or a virus that wreaks havoc on your computer. However, it affects you emotionally, rather than physically. By its very nature, a virus is weak until it has a host. Once it has a host, however, it replicates within that host and then spreads from one host to another. If you have anti-virus software protection on your computer system, an inadvertently downloaded virus probably will not infect your computer. But let us say your computer exhibits the effects of a virus that has changed its program to make it react in a certain way. Is it the computer that is causing the malfunction or is it the virus?

The same is true with your body. A virus does not naturally exist within the body; in fact, it cannot exist there if the body is healthy. When the mind or body is in a state of lowered resistance, a virus can impregnate your cells. The virus penetrates the outer layer of a cell, burrowing in and changing its DNA pattern. A cell or mind re-programmed by a virus will begin to respond in a way that the virus has been designed. Likewise, a Thought Virus cannot live in your mind unless your system is not protecting itself properly. So how do you protect yourself from Thought Viruses? Present Time Consciousness (PTC), which includes The Five Basics for Optimal Health of water, food, rest, exercise and owning your power.

Trigger-Thought Viruses enter the mind via the sensory passages you use to perceive the world in which you live. They are triggered by things you see, hear, smell, taste, feel or intuit. Say you are invited to a friend's house for dinner. Your friend has cooked spaghetti. As soon as you walk in the door and you smell the spaghetti sauce, you begin to feel fear. Maybe you walk into a music store. Mozart's Symphony No. 39 is playing and you are overwhelmed with anger and resentment. Or perhaps someone brushes against your arm, and suddenly you are feeling insecure.

Why does this happen? At some point during your life, you experienced a trauma or loss that was associated with a particular sense. When it happened, spaghetti sauce was cooking, or Symphony No. 39 was playing, or someone touched you in a certain way, and your feelings of fear, anger, resentment and/or insecurity were internalized on a subconscious level. This triggering of your senses caused your subconscious to forget about the present moment, and your body began to run the old pattern of trauma or loss. Your emotional and physical reactions go haywire; you feel as if you are spiraling out of control. However, it is not you. It is the Trigger-Thought Virus that has impregnated your DNA, causing you to react with emotions or feelings that have nothing to do with what you are actually experiencing.

96

Dysfunction is physiological as well as emotional, and thus affects our behavior, depending upon the code of the virus. It can cause all types of aberrant reactions on an emotional, structural or biochemical level, from headaches and muscle pain to indigestion and diabetes. Unless the Trigger-Thought Virus is recognized and then harmonized, the patterns will continue to run, affecting the body physiologically, emotionally and behaviorally.

A **Limiting-Thought Virus** causes you to believe that your potential to succeed has limits. It limits your potential to have good relationships, to be healthy, to be financially stable, to be creative, etc. Limiting-Thought Viruses are often spread by your closest relationships—parents, teachers, co-workers, bosses, friends and lovers—and they are planted when you are feeling vulnerable.

This is how a Limiting-Thought Virus works: Joey is doing poorly in math. His teacher tells him, "Joey, you're never going to be good at math! You just don't get it." Joey, whose dad is an accountant, has dreams of going into the family business. That, however, involves math. The Limiting-Thought Virus from his teacher infects Joey, who never pursues his dream.

David has his eye on a beautiful young woman. His friend says to him, "David, you think that girl would ever want to be with you? That kind of girl would never date you." Because David's emotional immune system is in a state of lowered resistance, he buys into his friend's point of view and allows the Limiting-Thought Virus to take over. Furthermore, whenever he sees a woman he feels is "that kind of girl," he never even attempts to talk to her.

I once had a guitar teacher who told my mother, "Don't waste your money on Darren; he has no talent for playing guitar." I was crushed; as a kid, I was so psyched about the possibility of playing in a band with my brother, who played the drums. Fortunately, I cleared that Limiting-Thought Virus and started playing guitar as an adult. I practice daily and I am actually quite good. At our wedding, I played guitar and serenaded my wife with a song I composed.

The most challenging Limiting-Thought Viruses I have treated as a holistic physician are those which allopathic doctors spread to their patients: "Mrs. Jones, you only have three months to live." "Everyone in your family has diabetes and hypertension, so you are going to get it, too." "No matter what you do, because you have big bones you will always be overweight unless you take this pill or have this surgery." It is as if cancer or autoimmune diseases automatically come with expiration dates. Patients immediately buy into it; they take in the Limiting-Thought Virus that is based on their doctor's beliefs. Who gave the doctor the virus? He got it from his teachers, his hospital training, his colleagues and his profession's Limiting-Thought Virus perspective on disease.

But bear in mind that there are infinite possibilities with every challenge. Though you may not be immediately aware of the solution, you should keep searching for the answer, no matter what the limiting beliefs of others.

When it comes to your health and making decisions about your treatments, you do have a choice. It is important not to assume that your doctor—any doctor—is right, that he/she has all the answers. You will find the answers to the health challenges you are facing within you. With The LifeLine Technique you are not only able to discover what the challenges are, but you also will be able to remove the limiting road blocks that are inhibiting your body from achieving optimal health. I do not treat viruses; I treat people. It does not matter what the diagnosis, your body has the capability and the potential to heal itself.

The **Killer-Thought Virus** is the most dangerous. It is a complex beast that challenges the mind in an extremely, self-destructive way. Killer-Thought Viruses are a combination of multiple Trigger-Thought Viruses and multiple Limiting-Thought Viruses. They cause complete breakdowns, both subconsciously and consciously, and lead to incongruent function in both the mind and body. They are the cause of suicide, both internal (lifestyle and behavior) and external (self-induced death). They literally program the person for death. For example, a woman in her early forties came to see me after being diagnosed with a rare form of cancer. The cancer was like a stealth plane, undetected by the immune system until it had progressed to an advanced stage. She had already undergone a bilateral radical mastectomy and a complete hysterectomy. During her first visit with me, I found and released three Killer-Thought Viruses having to do with anger, fear and low self-esteem associated with being sexually molested at the age of three. The Killer-Thought Viruses were the root causes of the cancer. The patient realized the relationships in her life that increased the potential for the Killer-Thought Viruses. She is doing her best to own her power and has begun to create the appropriate boundaries in those relationships.

The great thing about discovering a Killer-Thought Virus through The LifeLine Technique is that when the frequency is balanced, there are amazing shifts in a person's perception. There is a level of clarity that was not there before. All of a sudden, you will feel that your *reality* has returned and, for the first time, will become aware of a *new* reality of hope and opportunity.

The **Gemini-Thought Virus** is the shadow side of a person's life based on polar opposites, i.e., light/dark, yin/yang and good/bad. The Gemini-Thought Virus thrives on humiliation, shame, criticism and judgment. It creates the feeling that you are an abandoned, vulnerable child and unworthy of love. To overcome Gemini-Thought Viruses you must learn to accept all sides of yourself, rather than just identify with the negative or positive. The rose, for example, is beautiful, powerful yet fragile, and vibrant. It also has thorns that can cause injury. The thorns are the shadow side of the rose.

The Gemini-Thought Virus prevents you from total self-acceptance. If you have a habit of procrastination, the shadow side will say, "You're always late, and you'll never be on time to anything." Instead of looking at your life as a work in progress or that you have the potential to develop and improve your time management skills, you only focus on what you are lacking. Another example is when something wonderful occurs in your life and your shadow side says, "I just got lucky," rather than celebrating your efforts or hard work.

You attract the people you need in your life in order to heal your shadow side. It is the pendulum. As far as the pendulum will swing one way, it will swing back the same distance in the other direction. The Gemini-Thought Virus takes over when you do not own your power and live in PTC. The LifeLine Technique is a powerful tool for healing the shadow sides of yourself that limit you in multiple ways.

Emotional Cancer is another category of the Emotional Expression of The Five Elements. It is very important to understand that emotional cancer is not the same as cancer of the physical body. However, it can be a precursor and will result in cancer in the physical body unless it is harmonized. Cancer occurs when a normal cell mutates; the immune system is unable to recognize it, so it spreads or metastasizes. Emotional Cancer results when an emotion, such as anger is trapped within the subconscious mind. The emotional immune system becomes confused and is unable to recognize it, causing the mind and body to have a maladaptive stress response. The result is a mutation of the emotions and an emotional metastisis of the anger.

When the emotional immune system does not recognize the self from non-self, emotions begin to spread like wildfire. A person who is unable to manage anger, fear, grief or low self-esteem is expressing the symptoms of emotional cancer.

Fear mutated transforms into panic and anxiety. Anger will evolve into hate and rage. Low self-esteem will mutate into social phobias of seclusion and paranoia.

You have your own space and boundaries. Your space includes both your physical and your energetic body. Boundaries are based on your experiences. You use them to determine whether or not you feel safe. They are different for everyone, based on how much you are able to let yourself go and surrender to the moment. Based on familiarity or desire, you allow certain people within your space. **Personal Invasion** occurs when you feel your boundaries—emotional, physical, sexual or spiritual—have been crossed without your permission. How do you know when you are being personally invaded? You *feel* it as a level of discomfort when someone is around you. It is the tightness in your chest when you discover someone has re-arranged everything on your desk or someone has rummaged through your dresser drawers. It is a twinge in your stomach when someone other than your lover or family member stands too close to you. It is the flash of anger you feel when someone breaks into your car or home, steals your wallet at the gym, or says or does something offensive. An extreme level of personal invasion is rape.

In many ways, the collective karma of our nation is Personal Invasion. The Pilgrims personally invaded the Native Americans. Their space was everywhere; there were no boundaries or borders. They were a part of a collective, universal awareness that included sharing, living off the land, being reciprocal and appreciative. The European settlers invaded their space, putting up boundaries and property lines, stealing land, denying the humanity of the Native Americans.

Personal Invasion causes shock to the body. The result of the shock is that both emotions and the body lock up. Reacting in a fright, fight or flight mode, the mind "walls off" the memory. **Shock,** therefore, is a walled off area of emotion or energy. When the shock has been internalized, it manifests itself in other ways. One of its most prominent physical manifestations is allergies.

A child survives a fall from a magnolia tree that is in full bloom. After time, all of his broken bones heal. However, the shock of the accident is still rumbling through his body, so aberrant reactions on a physical and/or emotional level begin to occur. It may take years for the subconscious memory to be triggered. However, once it is tapped, the boy develops an allergy to flowers that begin to bloom in the exact month he first fell from the tree.

While it is true that environmental sensitivities are more common these days, allergies occur at a root level, where shock resides. Since September 11, 2001, coupled with the complete devastation of Southeast Asia by a tsunami and recently, Hurricane Katrina, I believe the entire world has been in shock. I have witnessed an increase in allergies, as well as other flu-like symptoms. It is not just the toxic environment, it is the toxic level of emotions that have been sealed off and denied. Those emotions seep out and are expressed in many ways, such as chronic pain, chronic organ dysfunction and chronic emotional relationship challenges.

Internalized emotion can be balanced with the power of Infinite Love & Gratitude. However, you need to take personal responsibility by living in Present Time Consciousness and by loving yourself unconditionally. Once Shock is identified, it takes one second to clear it and it is gone. Afterwards, it is important to make the necessary lifestyle changes to ensure that your body continues the healing process.

If you continue down the same life path you have always trod, you will keep getting the same results. Clearing the Shock is only the first step. It is not the magic silver bullet that kills the werewolf. If you find yourself in a situation where something reminds you of a loss or trauma, it is best to allow yourself to *feel* and observe the impact of that experience and *express* your emotions right then. By maintaining The Five Basics for Optimal Health—water, food, rest, exercise and owning your power—your body, mind and spirit will have all the tools necessary to handle the challenges you face.

The last area of the Emotional Expression in The Five Elements category is the **Life/Death Mode**. To understand this mode, imagine a light switch in your body. When the switch is turned on, your body is functioning in the Life Mode. When it is turned off, your body is functioning in the Death Mode. In the Life Mode, your body readily regenerates and heals. However, with certain losses or traumas, the switch can be turned off, causing your body to live in the Death Mode. In the Death Mode, your body begins a cycle that makes it susceptible to breakdown, which eventually will lead to degenerative disease and premature death. In the same sense, death is more apparent when life is diminished.

Disease is not added to the body; rather, health is taken away. You cannot add darkness to a room; you can only dim the lights. Because you are an electromagnetic being, you attract and repel experiences based on the conscious and subconscious polarity of your emotions. When you are in a Death Mode, you have a subconscious death wish that is draining your life force.

Let me give you an example. Something traumatic happens to you—you lose your job, your relationship ends or you are in a car accident. Or maybe you are hit by a Thought Virus while in a vulnerable state. All of a sudden, the proverbial switch of the subconscious mind turns off, and you are now living in a Death Mode. What does that mean? Every time a traumatic experience is subconsciously triggered, the reptilian brain sends out signals as if the trauma is actually happening. Your life and body literally begin to fall apart. As a result of the subconscious disconnection of past trauma, the trauma lives on by creating a death mode. There is a *part* of you that subconsciously wants and needs to be released. Not until the trauma is released will the body or your will to live change.

Autoimmune diseases occur when the body is in the Death Mode. Does autoimmune disease mean the body is attacking itself? If the body is naturally a self-healing organism then that answer does not make any sense. Instead, thanks to the field of psychoneuroimmunology, it has been proven that thoughts affect your nervous system, your immune system and hormonal regulation. Toxic thoughts trigger the body to switch to the Death Mode, propelling it to attack itself. My experience with patients has taught me that when the Death Mode is switched to the Life Mode, people begin to heal.

So if the body is talking in an autoimmune way, you have to ask why. Which belief systems, feelings or thought patterns are being denied that are forcing the body to live in the Death Mode? It is a difficult reality. On the other hand, what an opportunity to *awaken*! Rather than looking for the elusive "cure" outside yourself—i.e., support groups or medication, etc.—you can open yourself to the fact that the *cure is within you*. The greatest doctors in the world—lupus specialists or MS specialists—have not *cured* anybody. There has never been a pharmaceutical drug that has cured anybody of anything. The medications just get rid of the symptoms, which are the body's only way to communicate with you. There are other options.

The approach should not be "one size fits all," cookie cutter health care. It must be multidimensional in order to take into account the broad and ever-widening spectrum of realities that each individual experiences, internalizes and often manifests as illness. *Each journey to disease is different; therefore each path back to health must be tailored to the individual.*

CHAPTER SIXTEEN

Your Body's Structural Expression

The acupuncture meridians are integrated with every structural component of the body. Your body actually has a structural language that it uses when you have subconsciously internalized, denied or disconnected from your emotions. The specific meridian that has a decreased flow of life force will determine which structural aspect of the body will speak.

For three months, I experienced midline back pain which awakened me every morning at six o'clock. In addition to running The LifeLine Technique, I received acupuncture, cranial sacral treatments, massage, chiropractic adjustments, Applied Kinesiology and took additional nutritional supplements in order to help my body heal. The symptom would decrease; however, it always returned the next morning at 6:00.

During a massage on this area of my back, I had a memory of myself as an infant. I was born with bowed legs and was placed in a lower body cast to correct the structural imbalance. The cast kept my feet, legs and pelvis immobilized during the first year of my life. As my back was massaged, I realized how many dysfunctional emotional and physical patterns in my body were associated with this early life experience. Even though I adapted to the cast and developed upper body strength by pulling myself around with my arms, the cast inhibited the development of my natural cross-crawl pattern, planting seeds of imbalance.

It was also during the massage that I began to realize the subtle link between the pain in my back and other symptoms and traumas I had experienced throughout my life. For example, I recalled being in junior high and high school, wondering "how to walk." It was almost as if walking was not natural for me. I realized that rupturing my left Achilles tendon fifteen years later was also related. At the time, I was going through major turmoil in my life, and I was internalizing anger. The anger triggered subconscious memories of the original trauma of being stuck in the cast.

The hours of five to seven in the morning are when the large intestine acupuncture meridian is at its highest function. This is the time I woke up every morning with excruciating pain. Based on Applied Kinesiology, the area of pain in my back correlated with the muscles of the large intestine: the quadratus lumborum and the hamstrings. The back pain I felt can be likened to a ripened fruit, grown from the seeds planted during my infancy in the cast, and now ready for harvest. After running The LifeLine Technique on the memory of being in the cast, the back pain is now completely healed, and I have been pain-free since.

This experience is a great example of the interconnectedness of the Expression Channel on a structural level. When you find the boulder that has inhibited the natural flow of your river, it can be removed, allowing the body to do what it does best—heal.

Remember what Dr. Victor Frank says: "What you have is not what you've always got." What you have is a symptom. That symptom is the result of multiple autonomic reflexes that your body has produced throughout your life to warn you of imbalance. When we internalize, deny or disconnect from the emotions that are the result of challenging or painful experiences, the body expresses itself with symptoms.

There are all types of autonomic reflexes that exist in the body. One of which most people are aware is called the psycho-somatic reflex. Psycho-somatic means internalized emotions evolve into physical pain. For example, a woman came to see me who had been suffering for years with abdominal pain. No matter what she did, nothing alleviated the pain. Using The LifeLine Technique, her body released the internalized emotion of anger that she felt towards her mother. The harmonization of the internalized anger with Infinite Love & Gratitude enabled her body to heal.

There are other autonomic reflexes that travel and interconnect throughout the body. One is a viscero-somatic reflex. This reflex is stimulated when an organ is stressed, causing a signal to be sent to a specific part of the body, resulting in pain. Poor diet, dehydration, and toxicity will lead to a viscero-somatic reflex. For example, sugar is a poison that has the potential to cause viscero-somatic reflexes. An example of a viscero-somatic reflex is gallbladder dysfunction causing right shoulder pain. A dysfunction within the heart will result in referral pain down the left arm or into the jaw. Kidney stones cause back pain.

The somato-somatic reflex is caused by physical misalignment. This reflex is the result of overuse, direct trauma and poor posture. Chiropractic adjustments are a great way to balance somato-somatic reflexes.

Every organ in the body has a connection to the physical body in every possible combination. By recognizing these reflexes, the expression of a symptom takes on a whole new meaning. These autonomic reflexes exist within the body as a survival mechanism. They are produced to warn you that something is throwing you off balance. Without these reflexes, you would be unable to recognize that you have consumed too much sugar, are dehydrated, are not getting enough exercise, are lacking sleep, or are in a bad relationship. They enable you to recognize the complex matrix of the mind-body-spirit connection.

When we internalize, deny or disconnect from challenging experiences, the emotions that we are suppressing become stuck in different structural components of our bodies. The body holds on to internalized, denied or disconnected emotions in the muscles, joints, organs, fascia, lymphatics, circulation, nerves, integument, scar tissue, cartilage, fat tissue and bone. Any of these areas has the capacity to obstruct the body's ability to flow energetically. Treating the symptom will not heal the root cause of the pain. In fact, taking a medication, such as an anti-inflammatory or a painkiller, will result in your not being able to recognize that the imbalance still exists within a specific structure of the body.

The LifeLine Technique demonstrates a clear connection between the structural body and the acupuncture meridians of The Five Elements. When symptoms are expressed structurally, it is due to the subconscious internalization, denial or disconnection from emotions, causing a decrease flow in the body's life force within the body's various structures. Let us take a closer look to see the specific aspects of the way the body expresses itself structurally:

Muscle is the tissue of the body that primarily functions as a source of power. There are three types of muscle in the body. The muscle responsible for moving extremities and external areas of the body is called "skeletal muscle." Heart muscle is called "cardiac muscle." The muscle in the walls of arteries and bowel is called "smooth muscle." Muscles are where you store past memories, conflicts, experiences and feelings, including repressed anxieties, fear, guilt, and levels of self-worth, self-esteem, joy and vibrancy.

A **joint** is the area where two bones are attached for the purpose of motion of body parts. A joint is usually formed of fibrous connective tissue and cartilage. An articulation or an arthrosis is the same as a joint. Joints are grouped according to their motion: a ball and socket joint, a hinge joint, a condyloid joint, a pivot joint, gliding joint, and a saddle joint. The joints are the connections between thoughts and feelings and movement and action. They are the source of stability and balance in the body.

Organs are a grouping of tissues that are made up of specialized cells. Each organ has a specific function that is both independent of and interdependent with all the other organs. There are organs of digestion, respiration, elimination, reproduction, detoxification and assimilation, and they are the storehouse of your thoughts, feelings and beliefs. Every cell in the body is constantly in the process of regeneration and degeneration. There is a constant balancing between these cycles that will either influence the body towards health or disease. Each of the organs has corresponding emotions based on The Five Elements.

Fascia is the Latin word for "band or bandage." It is a flat band of connective tissue below the skin that covers underlying tissues and separates different layers from one another. Fascia encloses muscles and is where we express our need for protection.

The **lymphatic system** presents a network of vessels, nodes, and lymph-producing organs crucial to the body's immune response. The immune system determines that which is "self" and "not self" and then fights off intruders. Vital to locating and destroying these microscopic "intruders" are the T-cell lymphocytes, produced by the thymus gland, located near the heart. The spleen is also a source of lymphocytes. The lymph vessels collect the "drainage" of lymphocytes and macrophages (white blood cells) from the capillaries and then modify or return them to the blood system, draining into the veins near the heart. The new science of psycho-neuroimmunology studies the interaction of psychological factors (such as stress) with the immune system. With The LifeLine Technique, we can see the link between various personality factors and health. The lymphatic system also is the place in the body most closely linked to your identity and your ability to define your own thoughts and feelings, rather than having them defined by others.

The circulatory system moves blood throughout the body and is composed of the heart, arteries, capillaries, and veins. This remarkable system transports oxygenated blood from the lungs and heart throughout the body via the arteries. The blood also transports nutrients and waste products through the capillaries, which are situated between the arteries and veins. The blood that has been depleted of oxygen by the body is then returned to the lungs and heart via the veins. The blood represents the circulation of feelings of love and life.

The nervous system is composed of three parts: The central nervous system (CNS), the peripheral nervous system (PNS), and the autonomic nervous system (ANS). These three distinct parts integrate every function of every cell, organ and system of the body. It is through the electrical conduction of the nervous system that you are able to walk, breathe, think, feel and adapt to an array of extremes in many different environments.

The nervous system integrates all parts of an organism so that it is able to optimally function as a whole. It communicates via electrical currents that travel through synapses. Synapses occur when electricity jumps from one synaptic cleft to the next. It is very similar to telephone pole relay stations. When there is trouble with your telephone, the first place to check is your phone's connection to the wall outlet. If it is plugged in, the next step is to see whether there is a blockage along the telephone lines entering your home. If that checks out, assess the lines that feed your local area. And if those are clear, officials evaluate the city or main area where all calls are generated (the phone company). The final checkpoint would be the satellite sending the signal from outer space.

The same scenario is true in the body. The region expressing the symptom may be the location of the symptom's cause. Or it may be a communication breakdown from the symptom to another area in the body or mind. Finally, there may be an internal source that is causing the symptom to be expressed. There may be a relationship issue that is resulting in stored emotions, environmental pollution or poor dietary habits, leading to the symptom. It is usually a combination of all of these scenarios. Many symptoms can be associated with dysfunction in the nervous system. Numbness implies a withdrawal of feelings, perhaps because there is too much pain for us to absorb in that place. Numbness is a way of denying the pain, pushing it away or forgetting that part of ourselves. Nerve pain is a signpost showing us where we need to connect with psycho-emotional pain. It indicates that we are holding on tight, so we need to work at letting go.

Cartilage is a non-vascular structure found in various parts of the body. In adults, it is chiefly found in the joints, in the torso and in various tubes, such as air passages, nostrils and ears that are to be kept open permanently. In the early period of fetal development, the greater part of the skeleton is cartilaginous. Breakdowns in the cartilage are the same as for joints, usually implying a deep resistance or fear of movement.

Scar tissue is the end result of inflammation. "Itis" is the word that is used to describe an inflammatory disease process. Gastritis is inflammation of the stomach. Arthritis literally means inflammation of the joints. Every area of the body can have an "itis" added to it, denoting inflammation in that area. When inflammation persists, scar tissue is sure to form, creating an entirely new subset of challenges. The greatest of those challenges is that scar tissue does not conduct energy. Energy is the healing power that potentiates health and balance. Scar tissue that crosses acupuncture meridians inhibits the flow of *chi* (life force) through those meridians. So when scar tissue develops, there is a decrease in *chi*, which directly leads to a decrease in the circulation to that area. Remember, emotion is energy in motion. When scar tissue is present, all aspects of life force are inhibited, contributing to the internalized, denied or disconnected emotions remaining locked in the body.

The adipose or **fat tissue** of the body serves as an energy reserve. Subcutaneous fat provides an insulating layer that inhibits heat loss. Fat is an important constituent of cell structure, forming an integral part of the cell membrane. It acts to support and protect certain senses and organs, such as the eye and kidney. Fat tissue stores both emotional and physical poisons and toxins. As a person breaks down and metabolizes fat tissue, these emotional and physical poisons and toxins are released. If the detoxification routes are not open and there is dehydration in the system, the metabolism will slow down the breakdown of fat. Fat tissue is used to protect ourselves from internalized, denied or disconnected traumas. It is like a wall for protection against further hurt. At the same time, this blocks out feelings, which creates numbness to what is really being felt on the inside. If being overweight is an issue, the bigger we get, the more likely we are to reject ourselves and feel uglier and unlovable. Losing weight occurs through a deep shift in attitude, starting with an acceptance of ourselves just as we are—we need to give ourselves the love we long for, then we can start working on the layers of fear that lie beneath the excess weight.

Integument, or skin, is the largest organ of the body. Debbie Shapiro's book, *Your Body Speaks Your Mind,* describes it as "waterproof, washable, elastic, self-mending and tactile." It protects you against water loss and water intake, while allowing you to perspire; it defends you against infection and exposure to foreign substances; and it regulates your temperature. Shapiro says, "The skin is the outermost expression of (your) innermost being." Derived from the same primordial tissue as the nervous system, every feeling, emotion, belief and experience is registered through the skin. The acupuncture meridians and points are areas where energy is channeled reciprocally from the universe through the skin and into the depths of your being. Symptoms of the skin are often connected with communication difficulties and respecting boundaries.

Bone is the hardest structure of the body. It also possesses a certain degree of elasticity. The skeleton is created from bone. It provides the supportive inner framework of the body. Bone is the innermost core of yourself. The outside of bone is hard and dense, while the inside is porous and soft, filled with marrow. Bone marrow nourishes you with minerals, salts and nutrients, and produces vital immune cells, while the hard outer shell forms a strong, resilient framework upon which your whole being is built. Author Debbie Shapiro describes bones as the densest form of energy within the physical body; like the rocks in the earth, they support and sustain. The bones support your physical being and give life to the muscles and fluids. The same is true with your core beliefs giving you constant inner strength and support, while finding expression in your lifestyle, behavior and relationships. Imbalances or disease within the bones, therefore, represent conflict with the deepest part of your being.

The functional aspects of the human body's structural integrity are quite complex. The structural body begins to break down when it is forced to express the emotions that we have subconsciously compartmentalized. Knowing this, we discover the gift in the body's expression of structural pain or discomfort. We now can choose to use the power of Infinite Love & Gratitude to release the emotions that are inhibiting the body from healing and functioning optimally.

As technical as it may seem with each of these individual structural expressions, the treatment is simple—Infinite Love & Gratitude. Physical changes will occur instantaneously within the mind, body and spirit on a structural level when The Life-Line Technique is performed.

CHAPTER SEVENTEEN

Your Body's Biochemical Expression

Nothing is ever wasted in life. Just as in the law of conservation—energy can neither be created nor destroyed, it just changes form—the same is true within the body. The body is constantly keeping checks and balances of both its external and internal environment. This process enables the body to maintain balance in every moment. When the body is deficient, it will automatically begin to feed itself. When the body is in an excessive state, it will automatically begin to drain.

Every cell, organ, region and system is keeping tabs to maintain optimal health from a micro to macro perspective. For example, an ankle will lose energy when it is sprained. The body instantly responds to the deficiency of energy by swelling, which is its way of feeding energy to that area. Blood rapidly rushes to the ankle, as well as other fluids that contain minerals, nutrients and white blood cells to fight infection and help the ankle heal. Western medicine says rest, ice, compress and elevate a swollen ankle, which will then hopefully heal in seventy-two hours.

The LifeLine Technique, on the other hand, expedites the healing and enables the body to release and heal from an injury. On a root level, even twisting your ankle is caused by the subconscious internalization, denial or disconnection from emotions. Let me give you an example. I was having lunch in a restaurant with my office manager when our waiter came limping up to our table. We asked him why he was limping, and he told us that he had severely sprained his ankle one week before. He said that the pain, swelling and bruising had persisted and that he was very frustrated.

"Would you like to heal your ankle right now?" I asked him.

"Sure," he replied. "What would we need to do?"

"I'll be gently pressing down on your arm, and saying to your body, 'Infinite Love & Gratitude.'"

"Sure, let's do it," he said. "As strange as it sounds, that couldn't hurt me."

In the middle of the restaurant, I began to run The LifeLine Technique on him. It literally took me less than ten minutes. When I finished, I asked him to stand up, walk and check out his ankle. He noticed the difference immediately.

"Oh my God, this is amazing," he said as he walked around the restaurant without a limp.

I then checked The Five Basics for Optimal Health. I recommended that he increase his water intake and be sure to consume a gallon per day to satisfy his body's need for proper hydration. I also told him to follow The LifeLine Eating Plan, being careful to restrict his sugar intake over the next week in order to decrease any inflammatory response his body may be having. Lastly, I encouraged him to embrace this experience as an opportunity to learn and stay connected to the present moment.

Not only did The LifeLine Technique immediately enhance the self-healing mechanism for his ankle to recover, he also understood the emotions he was disconnecting from that led him to sprain his ankle. The body's capacity to heal itself is infinite. Stay in the moment and deal with the situation that you are in. The frequency of Infinite Love & Gratitude will harmonize and balance your body. The LifeLine Flow Chart will reveal where the energy in your body is imbalanced, why it is imbalanced and what is keeping it from healing instantly. The longer you stay disconnected, the longer it takes for the body to heal.

One of the major characteristics differentiating Western medicine from The LifeLine Treatment approach is the view of symptoms and disease. In Western medicine, fifty people all diagnosed with the same disease will be given the same medication or surgical advice. For example, with diabetes there are certain medications used to control blood sugar levels. As diabetes progresses and people develop retinopathies in the eyes or neuropathies in the extremities, there are specific surgical procedures that are then performed. A person will undergo multiple laser surgeries on their eyes for the retinopathies, and when the disease has progressed to the point of gangrene in the extremities, they will undergo amputation.

In The LifeLine approach, people that have been diagnosed with diabetes will be treated individually. The treatment plan will focus on where the primary imbalances are within the body. They will all be educated about the need to maintain The Five Basics for Optimal Health to allow their bodies to heal. The LifeLine practitioner will use muscle testing to assess regions, organs, glands, pathogens and systems and balance them on an emotional, biochemical, structural and spiritual level.

No two people treated with The LifeLine are treated the same exact way, because no two people are the same. No one has the same family, diet, lifestyle, trauma or losses. Every experience you have had in your life has shaped you to be where you are at this very moment. There is a subtle balance being maintained within your body at all times. Sometimes there is excess in one area while there is a deficiency in another. For example, when you have an excess of emotional stress due to insecurity, the emotion of fear within the body is elevated. The fear automatically will begin to drain the kidney acupuncture meridian causing the symptom of back pain. By taking medication for the back pain, you are doing nothing to alleviate the fear, the root cause of the symptom.

The LifeLine Technique will guide you through the flow chart like a laser, pinpointing the deficiency in the kidney acupuncture meridian. Through different layers of the original symptom of low back pain, The LifeLine Flow Chart will help the person recognize the insecurity and fear that is being internalized. Once recognized, The LifeLine practitioner will harmonize the insecure experience with Infinite Love & Gratitude. As a result, the body will have no need to express itself with low back pain.

Excess or deficiency can both lead to imbalance. The regulatory systems of the body are in a constant symphony of adaptation. When the energy of the body is running high, the mechanisms of the metabolism speed up to balance off any excess. The opposite is also true—when the energy of the body is running low, the metabolism slows down to store up energy and feed the body's deficient state.

I have a friend who is trained in using The LifeLine Technique. While at a coffee shop with his wife, a woman spilled a scalding cup of coffee on his leg. He instantly began sending "Infinite Love & Gratitude" to the area of the burn. The next day, the only sign of the accident was a small red dot. By draining the excess energy that was flowing because of the burn, his body was able to heal itself instantly.

The Biochemical Expression of The Five Elements is associated with the Creative (Shen), Destructive (Ko) or Connecting (Luo) cycles of the acupuncture meridians.

These cycles are inhibited when the acupuncture meridian is hypo-functioning or hyper-functioning. When the acupuncture meridian is hypo-functioning, it needs to be fed. When it is hyper-functioning, it needs to be drained. These actions allow the cycles to continue in a harmonious fashion and are accomplished easily using the power of Infinite Love & Gratitude.

Everything in the body happens for a reason. When you awaken to the subtle balance that the body is maintaining in every moment, you are empowered by the natural laws of the universe. There is a flow that exists within the universe, as well as within the body, that enables the body to maintain homeostasis. It is when you disconnect from your natural flow that your body begins to express symptoms. Symptoms can be the result of an excess or deficiency. Nevertheless, The LifeLine Technique brings the body back to balance.

CHAPTER EIGHTEEN

Breaking Out of the Holding Pattern

I had an eye-opening experience with a new patient. Melanie, age thirty-nine, was referred to me by her medical doctor for consultation and treatment. She was suffering from severe allergies and searching for another means to heal.

"I've had *my* allergies since birth," she explained to me during our first session. The list included several environmental allergies that limited her ability to eat and work. In addition to the allergies, she had chronic numbness along her spine and into her extremities, which debilitated her both physically and emotionally. Melanie sought the help of dozens of doctors over the years, but none of them were able to help her find relief.

As I listened to Melanie discuss the effects of the allergies on her life, I noticed a common theme of ownership shared by many people when it comes to illness. She took complete ownership of the allergies and the chronic pain as if they were threads of tissue connecting her skin. She wore them like badges. The symptoms and diseases that Melanie's body used to express itself had become her identity. I wondered if she was aware that so many relationships in her life were defined by this identity.

I began to run The LifeLine Flow Chart and within fifteen minutes of our session, the numbness immediately disappeared. By the time we finished, 90 percent of the symptoms were completely abated. For the first time in Melanie's life, she experienced a sense of inner health and well-being. Despite this new sense of hope, she was afraid.

"I don't know what to think of myself anymore," Melanie said.

I immediately knew she was talking about her identity, which had been stuck in a holding pattern of limiting beliefs and suffering. We created a treatment plan to detoxify Melanie's mind and body of the poisonous emotions and chemicals that were limiting her optimal potential. The mind and body must be detoxified before a person is able to heal.

Sometimes symptoms can become locked, like a tornado, into a continuous loop of imbalance. These are called holding patterns, the places where symptoms (disconnections from our emotions) become so deeply rooted in our lives that they become part of our being. Like airplanes in a holding pattern, the symptoms are stuck, waiting for air traffic control to give the green light for landing. The LifeLine Technique provides the means to land, to take the first step in breaking this loop by locating where the denial of our power is rooted. When the holding pattern is released, the body is able to restore balance.

Let us take a closer look at the various aspects of holding patterns. We have already discussed how our beliefs affect our health. I will now focus on other aspects of the mind: limiting beliefs, their origin and chakras.

As a result of The LifeLine Technique, I awakened to the connection between the universe and the body. The energy of the universe enters our bodies via the microcosmic orbit. The microcosmic orbit, otherwise known as the superconscious (or the Power Center in The LifeLine Flow Chart), is the main driver of our bio-computer. It is the *mind* of the body. The microcosmic orbit acts as an attractor field for emotions that are stored in the subconscious mind. It is the connection or liaison between the universe and the physical and emotional symptoms we experience.

The microcosmic orbit travels along two pathways. On the anterior of the body, it travels along the Ren Conception Vessel acupuncture meridian—beginning at the perineum, traveling up the midline of the body and ending at the inner aspect of the lower lip. On the posterior of the body, the microcosmic orbit travels along the Du-Governing Vessel acupuncture meridian, which begins at the tip of the tailbone, runs up the spine along the midline, continues over the head and ends on the inner aspect of the upper lip. These two vessels intersect in the soft palate, located in the roof of the mouth. When you use your tongue to touch the soft palate, it is like touching two wires together; these two energies ignite, instantaneously strengthening your entire system. This is why in meditation, tai chi and yoga, it is recommended that the tongue is kept pressed against the soft palate while breathing.

The microcosmic orbit produces an attractor field, an identifiable pattern, which emerges from our subconscious emotions. The microcosmic orbit is comprised of seven chakras. A Sanskrit word, "chakra" means *wheel* or *disk*. Each chakra moves with a spinning motion, forming a vortex. The vortices are the specific portals through which energy enters and exits throughout the body.

Each chakra is associated with the acupuncture meridians, physiological functions of the body, and beliefs or power. They correspond to a specific vibratory frequency, ranging from lower to higher along the spectrum of the rainbow. Think of the mnemonic, "ROY G BIV" (red, orange, yellow, green, blue, indigo and violet), as a way to remember which chakra corresponds to each color. The colors of the rainbow are created from the bending of light. Lower vibratory frequencies are observed at the end of the spectrum of red. As the frequencies increase in rate, the colors change sequentially into orange, yellow, green, blue, indigo and violet.

The chakras are like jellyfish. They have tendrils that simultaneously reach inward to the body and outward to the universe. They serve as magnets, attracting and repelling experiences that represent our subconscious mind. When you have subconsciously internalized, denied or disconnected from an experience, the energy that is attracted is of an aberrant frequency that affects the associated chakra. For example, limiting beliefs about self worth or value have a vibrational frequency that is channeled into the third chakra, which is yellow and is our connection to self-empowerment. Limiting beliefs associated with the third chakra will attract experiences such as abusive relationships or self-destructive behavior.

The assemblage point is a hole formed in the body's microcosmic orbit when the chakras are leaking energy. Our experiences are attracted through the assemblage point. By balancing the chakras with Infinite Love & Gratitude, the attractor field is balanced, closing off the assemblage point and securing the microcosmic orbit. When the microcosmic orbit is intact, you will no longer attract limiting experiences on all levels. Harmonizing the limiting attractor fields will enhance your health, finances, relationships and spiritual growth. However, you cannot idly sit by after limiting attractor fields have been harmonized. You have to take responsibility for the choices you have made and learn from the consequences.

The following is a chart of the chakras and their association with the body:

FIRST CHAKRA: ROOT—COLOR IS RED

Physical Issues: Lower back, sciatica, tailbone, rectum, colon, adrenals, feet, hands, and immune system.

Emotional Issues: Physical security; group safety and security; feeling at home; ability to stand up for oneself; stability with family, relationships, work and money.

Energy: All is one. Grounds the spirit with the body. Accept oneself and work on the physical plane in a loving way.

Root Chakra's Energy Will Leak: When you subscribe to family or social beliefs that no longer serve you. When you consider your religion, political beliefs, social class, etc., to be better than others. When you hold on to negative experiences with your family.

Root Chakra's Energy Will Be Reinforced: When you maintain a sense of pride in your ancestry and family traditions. When you draw on your family for love and support.

SECOND CHAKRA: SACRAL—COLOR IS ORANGE

Physical Issues: Genitals, reproductive organs, pelvic cavity, large intestine, lower vertebrae, appendix, bladder, hip area, wrists, and ankles.

Emotional Issues: Self vs. other; moving away from the tribe; pleasure surrounding sex, recreation, eating; physical and mental pleasures; power and control; blame and guilt; ethics and honor in relationships.

Energy: Honor one another. Use your creative forces. Be devoted to the self. Show integrity and honor within all relationships.

Sacral Chakra's Energy Will Leak: When you attempt to control others in relationships. When you fuel fears about making or losing money. When you hold unresolved conflicts about your sexuality.

Sacral Chakra's Energy Will Be Reinforced: When you go with the flow in relationships. When you release the power of money as a motivating factor. When you authentically express your sexuality.

THIRD CHAKRA: SOLAR PLEXUS—COLOR IS YELLOW

Physical Issues: Abdominal cavity, digestive organs, kidney, pancreas, liver, gallbladder, spleen, endocrine glands, calves, forearms, middle part of back and spine, and upper intestines.

Emotional Issues: Personal power, self-esteem, responsibility for making decisions, self-mastery, personal honor, sensitivity to criticism, and intuitive voice.

Energy: Honor oneself. Take responsibility for your choices and decisions. Learn to maintain strong personal boundaries in relationship to your tribal boundaries.

Solar Plexus Chakra's Energy Will Leak: When you break your commitments to yourself. When you manipulate others to gain their approval. When you fail to maintain clear personal boundaries.

Solar Plexus Chakra's Energy Will Be Reinforced: When you take pride in your work. When you trust your intuition. When you keep your word.

FOURTH CHAKRA: HEART—COLOR IS GREEN

Physical Issues: Heart center, circulatory system, chest, breasts, rib cage, lungs, diaphragm, thymus gland, knees, and elbows.

Emotional Issues: Love, failure, loneliness, disorientation, alienation, hatred, grief, anger, resentment, bitterness, forgiveness and compassion, hope and trust.

Energy: Love is divine power. Love yourself first and then others. Express love in actions. Release emotionally suppressed trauma. Be non-judgmental of others.

Heart Chakra's Energy Will Leak: When you allow past negative experiences to limit your choices. When you hold on to resentments. When you do not allow others to love you.

Heart Chakra's Energy Will Be Reinforced: When you forgive others unconditionally. When you love yourself. When you love others enough to let them experience the world in their own way.

FIFTH CHAKRA: THROAT—COLOR IS BLUE

Physical Issues: Throat, vocal cords, thyroid, parathyroid, and mouth.

Emotional Issues: Power of the will, judgment and criticism, outward expression and inward acceptance.

Energy: Surrender Personal Will to Divine Will. Express your truth—the power of the spoken word. Have the ability to speak.

Throat Charka's Energy Will Leak: When you let others define your needs and wants. When you tell lies. When you experience shame.

Throat Chakra's Energy Will Be Reinforced: When you exercise self-control. When you empower others. When you speak honestly.

Sixth Chakra: Third Eye—Color is Indigo

Physical Issues: Nervous system, pituitary gland, higher brain centers, eyes, ears, and nose.

Emotional Issues: Intuition, emotional intelligence, intellectual abilities, and openness to other ideas.

Energy: Seek only the truth. Have a balanced state of mind. See the truth and divine perfection in all things. Clear the subconscious in preparation for intuition.

Third Eye Chakra's Energy Will Leak: When you hold on to old grief. When you close your mind to non-rational possibilities. When you insist on rational explanations for your internal experience.

Third Eye Chakra's Energy Will Be Reinforced: When you take emotional risks. When you open your mind to extravagant possibilities. When you follow your hunches.

Seventh Chakra: Crown—Color is Violet

Physical Issues: Top of head, highest brain centers, pineal gland.

Emotional Issues: Faith, wisdom, spirituality, selflessness, ability to view situations from an expanded perspective, ability to trust life, and a sense of oneness with all creation.

Energy: Live in the present moment. Allow the spiritual doorway to remain open. Experience a connection with the divine.

Crown Chakra Energy Will Leak: When you live a life without faith. When you put conditions on your spiritual experience. When you reject guidance unless it comes in a form you approve.

Crown Chakra Energy Will Be Reinforced: When you pray consciously. When you express gratitude. When you regard your life as a vehicle for spiritual development.

Earlier we explored the ways your beliefs are influenced by your relationships with your parents, siblings, partners, teachers, religion, gender, race, age, media, and so on. These relationships are at the core of what creates the infrastructure of your values. In addition, your senses—vision, smell, hearing, taste, touch and intuition—influence your perception. Your perception of the external environment sends signals via the nervous system to every cell in your body. This signal enables the internal environment of your body to know what is going on in the outside world. This communication between the external environment and the internal environment provides your body with the greatest opportunity to optimally adapt to any experience with which it is confronted.

When you have internalized, denied or disconnected from any emotion, your mind or chakras will attract experiences that are associated with the original disconnection. Instead of seeing what you are actually experiencing, on a subconscious level you see the original experience from which you internalized, denied or disconnected. You know something is happening because you have uncomfortable feelings. However, on a conscious level you do not make the connection to the original traumatic experience. Your subconscious is keeping you stuck in a holding pattern of denial and disconnection because it perceives the experience as the original traumatic event. Not until the subconscious holding pattern is broken and a conscious awareness of the limiting belief has been made can you authentically respond to what you are actually experiencing.

For example, a child grows up with a critical parent for whom nothing ever seemed to be good enough and who never gave any praise. As a result, the child developed a limiting belief associated with self-worth or esteem. Or a child may have grown up with a parent who survived the Great Depression; a parent whose fears were forged by a lack of money or lack of food. As a result, that child developed a limiting belief about the need to horde beyond what is needed for survival. Both of these individuals hold the energy of limiting beliefs within their subconscious minds and will continue to attract experiences that reinforce those beliefs. The person with the limiting beliefs about self-worth will question his or her value in every one of his or her relationships, work, marriage, friends, etc. The person with the limiting beliefs about hording beyond what is needed for survival will attract experiences associated with never having enough money, food, clothes, etc. With Infinite Love & Gratitude and The LifeLine Technique, they can create a conscious connection to the subconscious limiting beliefs, breaking the holding pattern of suffering and victimization. Once the holding pattern of limiting beliefs is broken, they are able to embrace their greatness and the infinite potential that exists in each moment.

CHAPTER NINETEEN

Interrupting your Spirit's Journey

Are you connected to your feelings? Are you expressing them either through words or actions? For many of us, the answer is no. We have been conditioned *not* to feel, not to be authentic. We have disconnected. We have blocked the pain and are comfortably numb. The journey to awakening your spirit has been interrupted by limiting beliefs, imbalanced lifestyles, and loss or trauma.

Besides habit, I believe the primary reason for numbness is the fear of change or of falling out of balance, which often makes the fall harder. We have learned to operate on autopilot, shielding ourselves from discomfort in any way we can, in order to block our feelings or to keep ourselves numb. Emotional eating, excessive alcohol, overworking, shopping, sex, smoking and substance abuse are all ways in which we disconnect from our emotions.

When you deny pain, you deny your free will. Over a period of time, you disconnect from your ability to handle challenging experiences because you are unaware of what you are truly feeling. The more you shield yourself, the more you have to reconcile with anger, fear, guilt, shame, blame or low self-esteem that accumulates when you do not acknowledge your thoughts, feelings and beliefs. While the goal is not to wallow in painful emotions, I encourage you to acknowledge, experience and confront your emotions no matter how challenging.

The *Tibetan Book of Living and Dying* says, "Problems can be transformed into an opportunity for growth." You do not really have "problems"; you only think you do by the way you interpret a situation. Rather, a "problem" is a situation that creates an opportunity to react or respond in either a growth or a destructive manner. The "problem" is an illusion. It is a limiting perception of an experience. It is the perception of an experience without gratitude. Breaking the pattern of disconnection by staying connected to challenging experiences enables you to learn from the experience. Unless you learn from the experience, you will continue to make the same mistakes over and over again.

When you were in high school, if you did not pass algebra, you were unable to move on to trigonometry. You were required to retake algebra over and over again until you understood the material enough to pass the tests. Life is the same way. It provides multiple tests that you need to pass to move on. You will marry the same person, with a different face and name, over and over again until you learn the lessons of your previous relationship. You will continue to face the same financial challenges in business until you learn from the mistakes that you have made. You will be confronted with the same health issues over and over again until you take responsibility for the unhealthy lifestyle choices you have made.

Once you embrace an experience that you have internalized, denied or disconnected from, you will move forward to the next experience. In this way of flowing through life, there is no failure. Every problem, challenge and difficulty becomes the opportunity to learn, transform and create a new skill to awaken the spirit within you.

Just as water, sound and light travel in waves and particles, so does life. Sometimes the wave is traveling up and sometimes it is traveling down. Particles are particular moments we experience, such as the one you are having reading this book. The particle is the opportunity to feel and stay connected to Present Time Consciousness. Your thoughts, feelings and beliefs will create emotions and sensations within your body that guide you to the next moment, and the next, either carrying those particular thoughts, feelings and beliefs or creating whole new ones. The culmination of your moments will create a wave in either an upward or downward motion.

An infinite number of external factors can influence the flow of your life. Health issues, financial stress or relationship turmoil all can lead to stress that causes disconnection. This disconnection does nothing for the situation you are in; in fact, it leads to further challenges down the road.

124

Let us say you are traveling down your stream of life and instead of a particle coming your way, you get hit by a boulder. That boulder or traumatic experience goes beyond the scope of your ability to maintain balance and it sends you spinning beneath the surface of your river. You get caught in a whirlpool which sends you deeper. When you feel this current pulling you below, a natural reaction is to struggle against the pull of the current. It is best to let yourself go with the flow of the undercurrent. If you do, it will shoot you back to the surface, facing you in a safe direction once again. However, if you choose to struggle against the current, you may get sucked under and never come up again, or you may come back to the surface and be heading in a new direction that has even greater dangers in store for you. Instead of the boulder and the whirlpool, now you are heading in a direction that is leading you to a fifty-foot waterfall!

The boulder has changed and redefined your reality. You are no longer living in PTC—you are continuously reacting to the trauma. You might suddenly feel depressed, anxious, angry or fearful, or you might have chronic conditions such as constipation, sinus congestion, headaches, or back pain. Your body will continue to communicate these symptoms as long as necessary until the boulder is removed and you are reconnected to your spiritual path.

Ivan Pavlov was a physiology professor in Russia in the late 1800s. He is, however, best known for the contributions he made to the field of psychology with a study that discovered the effects of "classic conditioning" on behavior. Pavlov was observing the digestive process of dogs, doing his best to understand the connection between salivation and the action of the stomach.

His hypothesis was that they were closely linked by reflexes in the autonomic nervous system, but he was not exactly sure how. He set out to determine whether external stimuli affected the process. Initially, he starved the dogs to get them in a lower state of resistance. The dogs salivated when they saw and ate their food. Pavlov began to ring a bell at the same time that he fed them. After a while, the dogs began to salivate when they heard the bell, even if no food was present. In addition, Pavlov discovered that the dogs responded to what is called "differentiation of stimuli." He found that ringing different toned bells would also trigger the dogs to salivate.

In 1903, Pavlov published his results, calling this a "conditioned reflex," meaning a behavior that has to be learned. Although the focus of his award-winning life's work would remain physiology, Pavlov recognized that the discovery of "conditioning" could explain the behavior of psychotic people, especially those who withdraw from the world because they associate all stimuli with possible injury or threat.

Dr. Scott Walker, developer of the Neuro-Emotional Technique (NET), realized that the same principles of classical conditioning affect us as a result of an initial trauma. Building upon the work of Dr. Jennifer LaMonica, Dr. Walker demonstrated that we store the emotions of an initial trauma in our bodies, called a Neuro-Emotional Complex (NEC). When you see or hear something that recalls the trauma, even on a subconscious level, your reaction is similar to that of Pavlov's dogs and the bell; you return to the original event or trauma in a classical conditioning response. Trauma lowers the resistance of the body and creates an internal environment that is more susceptible to a conditioned response.

Addiction is an example of a conditioned response. It is a holding pattern in the spirit where you have been conditioned to numb yourself to pain. Whenever a situation triggers the feeling associated with an original trauma, the body yearns for an opiate release in order to numb the pain. The manifestation of addiction is different for everyone. The interesting aspect of the molecules of emotion in the body— neuropeptides—is that they bind to the same receptor sites as heroin. With this in mind, we are better able to appreciate the body's biochemical addiction to emotions.

Addiction is a symptom of longing to know one's truth but being afraid to do so. Addiction will inhibit the journey to awakening your spirit. It is the internalized fears of facing painful experiences that you have been conditioned to numb. Consciously or subconsciously, you hear the "Pavlovian bell" and instantaneously yearn to be numbed. You tell yourself that you are not addicted and have control. However, the subconscious mind feels discomfort and pain, and the rest is history. An addict will then do whatever is necessary to numb the pain.

We all have addictions and long to know our truth. However, when the original trauma is triggered consciously, or more commonly subconsciously, fear sets in. The bottom line is love—the loss of love, the taking away of love, denial of love, manipulation of love, lack of self-love. The initial trauma/boulder creates a limiting belief that filters our sensory perception and propels us into a cycle of addiction.

Linda, who is forty-seven, came to see me with a primary complaint of being addicted to sugar. She was stuck in a cycle that disempowered her. Once she began to eat sugar, she lost all control. I told Linda that before she gets to where she is going, she needs to be okay with where she is at. She needed to accept, both consciously and subconsciously, that she is a sugar addict. I had her state: "My name is Linda, and

I'm okay that I'm a sugar addict." Her muscle was strong when she stated her name; however, it went weak when she stated: "I am okay that I am a sugar addict."

We need to be okay and accept where we are presently, before we move forward. As I ran The LifeLine Flow Chart to this declarative statement, Linda's body began to tell the story of what had been keeping her locked into the addictive response to sugar. Her body revealed that she was internalizing fear from an emotional loss that had caused shock. The shock was being held by a limiting belief associated with her crown chakra, which occurred at the age of three years and six months. At that time, Linda first developed a limiting belief of being disconnected from a higher power or purpose due to a shocking experience. When her muscle went weak, the age of the initial trauma was revealed to be three years and six months. I could see from the expression on her face that she knew exactly what the original shocking experience was. Her arm went weak as she recalled the death of her father. He died in a tragic car accident. She had taken on her mother's fear of moving on in the wake of her husband's death. This internalized shock created an attractor field. Until Linda dealt with the shock of her father's death, she was trapped in a holding pattern of numbing internalized grief. Being addicted to sugar was the external experience that was attracted to the internalized grief. She numbed the pain of grief and fear by disconnecting with sugar.

The death of Linda's father masqueraded as a sugar addiction in Linda's limbic brain for forty-three years. Every time an experience was somewhat similar to the original occurrence of her father's death, the limbic structures of her brain would be triggered. This stimulation caused the limbic brain to attempt to send a signal to her neocortex. However, because Linda had subconsciously disconnected from the experience the signal was rerouted to the reptilian brain which kept Linda autonomically in a state of obsession, compulsion and ritualistic behaviors expressed as sugar addiction.

Whenever there is trauma, the direction a person is looking at the time of the trauma locks the memory in the subconscious mind. The specific eye direction is inhibited from processing the traumatic experience during sleep. Rapid Eye Movements (REMs) process experiences from the short-term memory banks into the long-term memory banks. When trauma occurs, REMs are inhibited, as a safety mechanism or a circuit breaker, to protect the person from being emotionally overloaded. The memory becomes locked in the eye movements, in a purgatory-like state. Dr. Francine Shapiro awakened to a technique that uses eye movement and other forms of rhythmical stimulation to help trauma victims. With Eye Movement Desensitization and Reprocessing (EMDR), she demonstrated how the brain can unlock painful memories and heal trauma.

The LifeLine Technique expands upon EMDR by determining the specific eye gazes locked out of REMs. By having a person follow my hand through different eye patterns, I recreate the exact number of REMs necessary to process the trauma into the long-term memory banks of the brain. The process of healing trauma is fast, non-invasive and reproducible. The LifeLine Technique is content-free, which means it is not necessary to share the traumatic experience to heal. Sometimes people share their memories, and other times they do not. Nonetheless, the release is clear in their eyes. The healing takes place with Infinite Love & Gratitude.

When a patient comes in with a specific symptom that The LifeLine Flow Chart indicates as being held in the spirit/electromagnetic field, the symptom is released from the spiritual body through synthetic REMs. Synthetic REMs free the traumatic memory that has been locked away, releasing the memory to be processed by the brain's cortex. The synthetic REMs reconnect the spirit's flow to the will of the person, while at the same time, reconnecting his or her mind and body. Once reconnected, that person will release the traumatic incident without having to re-experience the pain of the trauma.

During the second layer of the treatment with Linda, I discovered the direction in which she was looking at the time she learned of her father's death. She was looking down and to the right, which kept her brain in a holding pattern and inhibited the REMs in that direction. The lack of REMs prevented the conscious processing of the grief and fear related to Linda's traumatic childhood experience. Finding and processing the specific eye movement made it possible to create a conscious connection to this subconscious experience and help Linda release the addiction to sugar.

The addiction to sugar was a gift that enabled Linda to embrace the emotions from which she had disconnected. Using muscle testing, I discovered which of the Five Basics for Optimal Health on which Linda needed to focus. By maintaining a healthy eating program, regular exercise and owning her power, she would be equipped to reconnect to her feelings of grief and fear that *caused* the sugar addiction. Linda left the office smiling, lighter and empowered to embrace her truth.

Feelings that are buried alive never die. Every challenge provides us with an opportunity to heal and to achieve our highest potential.

CHAPTER TWENTY

Discovering the
Pearl in the Oyster

In the beginning was the word, and that word was Love. The vibratory frequency of Love is infinite; it is the interconnection of everything. When I speak of the collective conscious or universe, I am referring to Infinite Love, to which we are always connected. When we choose to view life in a limited way, we are disconnecting from Infinite Love.

Thanks to modern science, we understand the human body in a detailed way, both anatomically and functionally. The same is now true of the electromagnetic field, which surrounds the body and vibrates with varying frequencies of light and energy. Kirlian photography and other scientific means enable us to view and understand the human electromagnetic field.

Emotions begin as an energetic frequency. This frequency originates from the collective conscious or universe. When we have a particular experience, that frequency is filtered into the body through the microcosmic orbit creating specific thoughts, feelings and beliefs that the brain categorizes and integrates. The brain translates these frequencies into images, voices, pictures and memories that connect the electromagnetic frequency to the physical realm, or the spirit to the body.

When these images, voices, pictures or memories are painful or uncomfortable, we will sometimes subconsciously disconnect from them. We know that the cause of symptoms is the disconnection from our emotions. The disconnection begins in the microcosmic orbit. That disconnection is called the Assemblage Point.

As mentioned earlier, the microcosmic orbit consists of seven chakras, and these chakras, which appear as spirals or vortices, trace vertically through the spinal column. Although the microcosmic orbit seldom appears to be visible to the untrained eye, it is as real as the light from the sun, radio waves or x-rays.

Life begins as energy and then potentially manifests into the physical realm. The Assemblage Point is the anatomical location in the energetic field where we have initially disconnected from our emotions. The Assemblage Point is like a pearl in an oyster. It is the treasure that is bestowed upon us when we embrace the original painful or challenging experience from which we have disconnected.

Pearls are not formed by a natural process inside an oyster. Natural pearls are formed when an accidental intruder enters a mollusk's shell. To defend itself, layer after layer of a substance called nacre grows and forms like onion skins around the particle. These are semi-opaque layers that consist of calcium carbonate that make up the pearl and become a coat for the particle.

Inevitably, natural pearls vary because the process depends on the shape of the piece being coated by nature. A process was developed to imitate natural pearl formation, creating "cultured" pearls. Like natural pearls, cultured pearls grow inside a mollusk, but with human intervention. Shells are carefully opened and different shapes of beads are inserted. Over time the inserted beads become coated with nacre, which makes a pearl appear to glow inside and gives it a beautiful shine.

This same process occurs with experiences that are painful and challenging to human beings, except we do not have the pearl to show for it; we have a symptom. When we disconnect, internalize or deny a painful or challenging experience, a process is set into motion. The sand, or the painful experience, is the disconnection or the Assemblage Point. It creates a layering around that moment which grows in its own unique fashion, depending upon the nature of the painful experience itself. Just like the pearl, the longer an experience has been denied, the more layers form around that original experience. At the same time, the more layers there are, the greater the opportunity to heal; the greater the gift.

The symptom begins to grow, like a pearl, when it is ignored. It begins subtly in the microcosmic orbit as an uncomfortable thought, feeling or belief that will continue to create layer after layer until it is removed. If the pearl stayed within the oyster and continued to grow for too long, the oyster would die. The same holds true for symptoms. By internalizing, denying or disconnecting from a symptom, it develops the potential of having so many layers that it will destroy the body. Embracing uncomfortable emotions—your pearls—enhances the health of your spirit and body, and opens your life to Infinite Love.

As you now know from Dr. Emoto's work, living your life with the attitude of gratitude literally changes the molecular structure of water that makes up your body. Being grateful is an act of courage and trust that the universe is perfect. Considering that you are a manifestation of the universe, every experience you encounter has a reason. Your challenge in life is to embrace whatever comes your way. From your very first breath to your very last, life is painful and challenging. It is by embracing the pain and challenges with gratitude that you choose not to suffer.

The meaning and purpose of life is discovered in the process of overcoming life's challenges with dignity, courage and faith. We all have the choice to discover "the pearl" in the oyster of life. Grab it with both hands and embrace the beauty of the experiences that your life is offering you.

Part Two

Owning Your Power

Let my life force be linked to my heart.
Let my heart be linked to the truth in me.
Let that truth be linked to the eternal,
that eternal, which is unending bliss.

Laghn Nyasa Upanishads

CHAPTER TWENTY-ONE

The Power to Create A Healthy Life

What is health? The word "health" is a derivative of wholeness and healing. It means a state of complete balance and harmony. The source of true health is maintaining balance on an emotional, structural, biochemical and spiritual level. Our bodies are miraculous self-healing organisms built to monitor anything that happens. For example, when we cut ourselves, white corpuscles instantly rush to the spot to fight infection while the platelets congeal the blood and seal up the cut. It all happens automatically; we do not have to think about it. Our body already knows exactly how to repair itself, just as it knows how to extract nutrients from food and dispense it as energy to various parts of the body.

In order to create the optimal conditions for your body to take care of itself, you must be proactive in your efforts. You must accept *complete responsibility* for your health. The LifeLine Technique provides the tools necessary to restore the body's balance and facilitate optimal health.

Taking care of yourself means more than watching your weight. It means becoming intuitively attuned to the subtle and sophisticated ways in which your body works so that you are aware and can respond when it is out of balance. It means understanding how the internalization, denial or disconnection from your emotions creates the conditions for lack of health. It means understanding that feeling sick is not a bad thing, but rather it is the body's way of saying that it is time to take responsibility and heal. It means consciously eating wholesome foods, drinking pure water, exercising, getting enough rest and owning your power. The LifeLine Technique is the best possible tool for rebalancing the body so that it will heal itself. However, to facilitate the healing process, you must maintain a healthy lifestyle.

The Five Basics for Optimal Health are:

✓ **Water**
✓ **Food**
✓ **Rest**
✓ **Exercise**
✓ **Own Your Power**

For each of these components, there are three aspects:

➢ **Quantity**
➢ **Quality**
➢ **Frequency**

Each of The Five Basics for Optimal Health are explained in depth on the following pages, including some guidelines on how best to use them.

You do not have to be a doctor to understand your body. Nor do you have to understand every aspect of holistic health care. The most important things you can do to develop optimal health are to stay in Present Time Consciousness, pay attention to what your body is telling you, set goals and take steps to achieve them.

According to the science of Psycho-Cybernetics, you have the power to program yourself for success. Dr. Maxwell Maltz, a plastic surgeon, is credited with discovering Psycho-Cybernetics, which is the application of the science of Cybernetics (goal-oriented behavior of mechanical systems) to human behavior. Dr. Maltz contends that "positive thinking" only works when it is consistent with your self-image, which is based on your experience, rather than intellectual knowledge. Consequently, for The Five Basics for Optimal Health to effectively help you improve the quality of your health, you will have to go beyond reading this book; you will have to take action!

Dr. Maltz writes in his book, *Psycho-Cybernetics*, that it usually requires a minimum of nineteen days to affect any perceptible change in your mental image. And to make it happen, he says, you have to have a plan. Dr. Maltz recommends five steps to achieve success, which he defines as the ongoing *process* of achieving a goal:

1. Your built-in "success mechanism" must have a goal that you conceive of as "already in existence—now." For example, during the process of writing this book, I maintained a vision of this book as a bestseller.

2. The automatic mechanism is teleological—it must be oriented to "end results." The means to achieving the goal will become clear in the process.

3. Do not be afraid of making mistakes or of temporary failures. You will achieve goals by paying attention to negative feedback and by going forward, making mistakes, and immediately correcting your course.

4. Skill learning of any kind is accomplished by trial and error, mentally correcting your aim after an error until a "successful" motion or movement has been achieved. After that, forgetting past errors and remembering successful responses are the keys to continued success, so that it will be replicated.

5. Learn to trust your creative mechanism to do its work and not "jam it" by becoming concerned or anxious about whether or not it will work out. Go with the flow and *let it work*, rather than *make it work*.

The key to activating your "success mechanism" as it relates to your health is visioning. When you close your eyes and think about yourself as a healthy person, what do you see? What do you look like? What do you feel like? What is the qualitative difference between now and the "new self" you are creating?

Take a moment and write down your vision of health. As you integrate The Five Basics for Optimal Health into your daily life, use your written vision as a source of motivation to stay on track. If you need more than written words, I recommend the *visioning* techniques outlined by noted art therapist, Lucia Capacchione, Ph.D., in her book, *Visioning*. Because "life is a work of art, designed by the one who lives it," Dr. Capacchione recommends creating a collage of images, symbols and words to support your vision of what you want your life to be.

No matter which path you choose, be courageous, follow your heart and intuition, and keep moving. Julia Cameron, author of *The Artist's Way*, once said, "Leap and the net will appear." The only mistake you can make is not doing anything at all.

CHAPTER TWENTY-TWO

Water: The Essential Component of Optimal Health

Visualize a constantly flowing stream. Notice how the water is moving, pushing all obstructions out of the way. Now think about a retention pond with stagnant water. Notice the debris, scum, algae and mold rising to the surface. Look at the pathogenic life beginning to form. The more water you drink, the stronger the flow of your internal stream, making it difficult for pathogenic organisms and disease to take root in your system. I am sure you have heard this before: you can live without food, but not without water, making it an essential component of optimal health. Water plays a role in nearly every bodily function—from regulating temperature and cushioning joints, to bringing oxygen to cells and removing waste from the body.

Your body is composed of 75 percent water and 25 percent solid matter. Brain tissue is 85 percent water; blood is 82 percent water; and the lungs are nearly 90 percent water. The body is like a sponge and is composed of trillions of cells that absorb and hold water. According to the late Dr. F. Batmanghelidj, a medical doctor and author of the book, *Your Body's Many Cries For Water* (www.watercure.com), the need for water is an essential part of human evolution:

When the human body developed from the species that were given life in water, the same dependence on the life-giving properties of water was inherited. The role of water itself in the body of living species, mankind included, has not changed since the first creation of life from salt water and its subsequent adaptation to fresh water.

Because water conducts electricity, it is not safe to hold a hair dryer or radio while standing in a bathtub or to swim during an electrical storm. However, as an electrical being, you need water for conductivity to facilitate the operation of all of your body's major functions—thinking, circulation, breathing, and elimination. As the primary conductor of electricity, water carries the necessary electrical charges (information) to every cell in the body; every cell in the body is dependent upon water to function optimally. If that channel is blocked in any way, the body will not function properly.

Dehydration is the condition in which the body's ability to function as a self-healing organism is blocked. Dehydration will affect blood pressure, blood sugar metabolism, digestion and kidney function. Thirst means the body is already dehydrated; dry mouth is the last symptom of chronic dehydration.

What causes dehydration? Besides the fact that many people do not drink enough water, they also drink excessive amounts of coffee, sugar-filled coffee drinks, regular and diet soda, herbal and regular tea, sports drinks and concentrated juices. Sugar dehydrates the body. Caffeine is a diuretic that causes the body to eliminate fluids. Have you ever felt foggy and even after drinking a cup of coffee or tea, your mind still was not clear? It is likely the mental fog was initially caused by *dehydration*, and the coffee or tea made it worse.

Most of us think of thirst as the common signal that our bodies need water. However, because we have ignored our thirst signal or responded with fluids that make the situation worse, we have become desensitized. This speeds up the aging process. Consequently, as we age, we gradually lose our perception of thirst, compounding the challenge. Fatigue is the first symptom of dehydration. By the time we feel thirsty, we are already dehydrated. In addition to fatigue, pain is another sign the body sends that it needs more water.

Dr. Batmanghelidj's extensive research on the effects of dehydration, detailed in his book, has determined that many common ailments are actually the result of not drinking enough water, including:

❑ Morning sickness in pregnant women
❑ Allergic sensitivities
❑ Heartburn
❑ Colitis
❑ Rheumatoid Arthritis
❑ Fibromyalgia
❑ Back Pain
❑ Angina pain
❑ Migraines and other headaches
❑ Depression
❑ Leg pain when walking
❑ Obesity
❑ High blood pressure
❑ High cholesterol

The United States Food and Drug Administration's healthy eating guidelines recommend a minimum of eight glasses of water (64 ounces) a day. However, Dr. Batmanghelidj recommends that we drink a lot more than that—half of our body weight in ounces of water. For example, a 180-pound person would drink 90 ounces of water. My experience has shown that optimal health will best be achieved and maintained when we drink one quart (32 ounces) of water for every 50 pounds of body weight, rounding up to the highest quart. For example, a 180-pound person would need to drink four quarts of water or 128 ounces of water on a daily basis.

Hot weather or exercise increases the body's required needs for water. If you drink coffee, tea (herbal, black or green) or juice, be sure to also drink an equal, additional amount of water for every ounce you consume of these other beverages so that your body will be fully hydrated. There is no nutritional value gained from drinking soda or any other sugar or artificially sweetened beverage. Even water with a slice of lemon is a diuretic and therefore increases your daily water requirement.

Water is best consumed at room temperature and sipped all day long. It is best to drink water that is free of chemicals, bacteria and heavy metals. Because of this, bottled or filtered water is preferable to tap water. The challenge I have with bottled water is that it is dead. There actually is an experation date on bottled water. By the time it is consumed the water has lost its oxygen and vitality from its source. Every bottled water that I have personally evaluated with pH strips reveals acidity. An acidic water will lead to inflamation in the body and chronic inflamation either localized or systemic will result in some form of degenerative disease. In addition to the cost factor, researchers have found that certain plastics will leach chemicals into the water, causing other health challenges. Chemicals in certain plastics have been found to bind to the same receptor sites as hormones, thus creating hormonal imbalances. As cited in the April 2003 issue of *Current Biology* (13:546–553), researchers found that even extremely low levels of the compound called Bisphenol A (BPA), produced genetic abnormalities. The journal reported that BPA exhibits hormone-like properties and imitates the effects of naturally occurring estrogens.

Dr. Joe Mercola, a noted holistic physician, recommends purchasing water in either clear, polyethylene, five-gallon containers or water from the grocery store that is sold in the clear bottles (polyethylene) because they do not transfer chemicals into the water (the cause of that awful plastic taste of the water in many cloudy-plastic bottled varieties).

The filtration system that I personally use utilizes PiMag water filtration technology. I have found through muscle testing that PiMag water consistently increases the strength of everyone that I test. PiMag water has a consistent pH of 7.4, therefore it is alkaline. An alkaline environment is essential for maintaining balance and optimal health. Disease such as cancer thrives in an acidic environment.

PiMag water was discovered in 1964 by Japanese botanists. They noticed that near a small town in Japan, a narrow stream flowed between two hills. One hill was largely magnetite; the other contained calcium compounds, which produced ions with a net positive charge. The stream between them coursed over a bed of silicates, the material that forms natural crystal. The combination produced negative ions.

These scientists noticed that the water in this stream had remarkable effects on the surrounding plant life. They set out to reproduce this natural water in a laboratory. As a result, an enhanced system of water filtration was developed, which is known as Pi-Mag water technology. This system adds several components to the water, including the benefits of magnetic and far infrared energy.

The primary stages of Pi-Mag filtration include a stainless steel screen and carbon filters. Carbon has been used for decades in scientific labs to remove impurities. Porous coral sand chips make up another layer of natural, non-chemical filters to remove contaminants and improve taste. Particles, as small as 1/10 of a micron, are trapped during an ultra filtration stage, which is based on the technology used in kidney dialysis. The pore size is the smallest in the industry. A third process filters water through clay ceramics and stones, reflecting far infrared energy and several minerals, including calcium to the water.

In addition to all the micro filtration, the water is energized and enhanced as it flows through powerful magnets, ceramic magnetite stone, oxidative stone, and pH stabilizing stone.

The work of Dr. Masaru Emoto, as mentioned earlier, demonstrates that water has consciousness, as well as other *life-giving* qualities. Dr. Emoto, whose work is documented in Volumes One, Two and Three of the book *Messages from Water*, began by studying the crystallization process of water as it passed from liquid into a freezing state. He extracted crystals from various vials of water and studied them under a dark field microscope that had photographic capabilities. He soon realized that the nature of the crystals was based upon the source of the water, i.e., natural springs, city water systems, snowflakes and stagnant ponds of water. This discovery made Dr. Emoto curious to see whether the frequency of words or sounds would have any impact on water. Through repeated experiments exposing vials of water to spoken and written words, as well as to music, he demonstrated how thoughts and words alter the molecular structure of water.

One of the most profound of Dr. Emoto's experiments involved a group of instructors from all over Japan. He told them he would be placing a cup of ordinary tap water on his desk at a specific date and time and he asked them to transmit their feelings to that water—to send *"chi* and soul" of love—and to wish that the water would become clean.

Tap Water Before   **Positive Thoughts of**
Positive Intention   **Chi, Soul and Spirit**

On January 17, 1995, the Great Hanshin-Awaji Earthquake occurred in Kobe, Japan. Three days later, Dr. Emoto took photographs of the crystals found in the tap water in Kobe. It was as if the water captured the fear, panic and deep sorrow of the people immediately after the earthquake. The crystals were completely destroyed.

He extracted crystals of water before and after the cup was placed on his desk. The transformation of the water was astonishing, confirming the power of *thought* on water.

We live on a planet that is more than 70 percent water. Our bodies are comprised of 75 to 90 percent water. The implications of Dr. Emoto's work are astonishing, not only for health, but for the well-being of the entire planet.

**Immediately
After Earthquake**

People from around the world helped with the reconstruction of the city. The citizens of Kobe received praise and blessings for coming together in a time of crisis. They transformed the tragedy of the earthquake into an opportunity to unite their efforts for restoring their home. This crystal, extracted three months after the earthquake, seems to have collected those feelings.

**Three months
After Earthquake**

We have the power to change the structure of water through our thoughts, words and actions. It means we have the power to change the course of our health through our thoughts, words and actions. The efficacy of The LifeLine Technique is based on the premise that "Infinite Love & Gratitude," whether written, spoken or reflected in someone's actions, has tremendous power to heal.

As we now know from Dr. Emoto's research, not all waters are equal. The energy of the water you drink determines the health-giving properties it has for the body. It is now understood that water can be damaged by several factors, including the environment, the emotion of the people living in the environment, music, the pressure in pipes, the pressure from water pumps, straight-line water pipes or conduits (in nature, water curves and spirals), exposure to negatively charged chemicals, heavy metals or other contaminants. The combination of these factors results in the loss of water's charge, or vibratory rate.

For optimal health, do not drink unfiltered tap water! The chlorine and fluoride used to "purify" the water are toxic chemicals and have been known to cause severe health challenges. Many houses have lead or copper pipes; the heavy metals from the pipes immediately go into the water. Tap water can also contain many toxins, pesticides, and bacteria.

The bottom line is to do the best you can with what you have. No matter what type of water you are drinking, writing "Infinite Love & Gratitude" on the container increases the energetic quality of that water. Structure is directly related to function. Infinite Love & Gratitude enhances the pure crystalline structure of water, thus increasing its functional healing potential.

CHAPTER TWENTY-THREE

Kicking The Sugar Habit

Sugar is the biggest *drug* scandal in the world today. Used for its taste and/or as a preservative, sugar is highly addictive, has no nutritional value, is high in calories, is poisonous to the system and prompts the body to enter a degenerative state because it leads to insulin sensitivity. Sugar abuse is epidemic and catastrophic; instances of diabetes and obesity, especially for children, are out of control.

SYMPTOMS AND ILLNESSES RELATED TO EATING TOO MUCH SUGAR

Mood Swings	PMS	Rashes
Poor Concentration	Memory Loss	Chronic Fatigue
Headaches	Spaciness	Arthritis
Sugar Cravings	Vaginitis	Irritability
Menstrual Problems	High Cholesterol	High Triglycerides
Obesity	Fibromyalgia	Frequent Colds
Diabetes Mellitus	Yeast Infections	Running Ear
Depression	Low Libido	Joint and Muscle Pain
Allergies	Epilepsy	Low Back Pain
High Blood Pressure	Migraines	Cardiovascular Disease
Hyperactivity	ADD	Learning Disabilities

Courtesy Dr. Jacqueline Paltis, author, *Sugar Control Bible and Cookbook*

If you do not add refined, cane sugar to your coffee, tea or cereal, or if you are a vegetarian or a vegan, you may think this does not apply to you. It is time to take off the blinders. Sugar reactions can be triggered by *any* food that breaks down in the body in the same way. When we talk about sugar, the list includes white *and* wheat bread, whole grain and white flour, pasta, crackers, cereals, all potatoes, brown and white rice, popcorn, and tofu. *All* simple carbohydrates, refined foods, processed foods and starches result in a massive insulin secretion that breaks down these foods so that your body can use them.

No matter what your eating regimen, most of the diets today are too high in simple carbohydrates: enriched and whole grain refined flour (bread and crackers), pastry, pasta, rice, concentrated sweeteners (sugar, fructose, and honey), ice cream, even ketchup. Carbohydrates, simple and complex (especially potatoes, dried beans, grains), ultimately break down into simple sugars. Digested and assimilated rapidly by the body, these sugars can provide quick, short-term energy, raise the blood sugar level and stimulate the production of insulin. Carbohydrates are beneficial when eaten in the form of whole fresh fruits and vegetables with all of the fiber intact. Fruits and vegetables contain vitamins, minerals, enzymes and antioxidants. They also are alkaline and help neutralize the acidity of animal protein.

If we eat too many carbohydrates or not enough protein, our body becomes imbalanced. Sugar cravings are a symptom, just like a headache, and a sign of imbalance in your sugar metabolism. They are a sign of a breakdown in communication between the systems responsible for maintaining the balance of your sugar metabolism.

Almost every person who enters my office is struggling with some aspect of insulin sensitivity and sugar imbalance. That means one or all of the three organs that are partners in the process—the liver, pancreas and adrenal glands—are very likely in crisis. Although we have been taught that blood sugar metabolism challenges are the result of the improper functioning of the pancreas, this is not true, except in the case of Type 1 diabetes.

The liver communicates and serves as the modulator between the pancreas and the adrenal glands. It is your liver that is responsible for telling the pancreas how much insulin to secrete in order to handle the meal you have just eaten. Your liver continues to monitor the situation to ensure that the blood glucose levels have decreased. Then it sends a message to the adrenal cortex to secrete enough glucocorticoids to raise your blood glucose and maintain an even feeding of nourishment to the brain.

According to Dr. Jacqueline Paltis in *The Sugar Control Bible and Cookbook,* Johns Hopkins University conducted a study in which the cadavers of 5000 diabetics were autopsied. Only 2 percent of the bodies examined had a degenerated pancreas. However, 98 percent had liver disease. What does that say about diabetes? It is a liver disease. How does the liver play its role? Let us look at a typical person whose diet consists of sugar and carbohydrates. This person, on an average, eats two meals per day. After lunch, he is feeling a bit sluggish, so he eats a candy bar and drinks a can of diet or regular soda. Inside his body, all of the communication channels are shut down until he eats and there is an alert that there is glucose in the system. The liver has been asleep, and the infusion of glucose startles the liver awake.

"Wow!," thinks the liver. "Look at all this glucose!" The liver immediately says to the pancreas, "Why aren't you secreting insulin?"

"You never sent me the message to do that," the pancreas responds.

"Just do it now!" the liver exclaims.

"Okay!" the pancreas yells back. It opens all of the channels and the system is flooded with insulin.

"Red alert!" the liver screams. "Mayday! Mayday!"

The gush of insulin causes the blood glucose to plummet. Meanwhile, the liver falls asleep again. The man whose body is going through all of these changes goes into a hypoglycemic reaction and is more fatigued than ever. The liver is startled awake again and it begins yelling at the adrenals.

"What's the matter with you?" the liver demands. "Why haven't you secreted any glucocorticoids?"

"I never got the message from you," the adrenals exclaim.

"Well, I'm telling you now!" the liver snaps back.

The man has a burst of anger and the adrenals open all of the channels, flooding the body with a burst of glucocorticoids. The glucocorticoids lead to a raising of blood glucose levels, and the man is now in a hyperglycemic (too much blood sugar) roar. It is an endless cycle until the liver, pancreas or adrenals shut down in exhaustion, waving a white flag!

Dr. Jacqueline Paltis, author of *The Sugar Control Bible and Cookbook,* writes that blood sugar malfunctions are the result of a communication breakdown:

The liver cannot maintain the feedback loop (a kind of running dialogue) that lets the pancreas and adrenals know the blood glucose status. Methionine (an amino acid) is the chemical messenger in this communication, but the liver does not have enough of the right kind of methionine to do the job. . . . In addition, methionine is the limiting amino acid (kind of a smallest common denominator) for the liver to process both sugar and protein.

L-methionine is most highly prevalent in red meat, essential in Western diets in order to maintain a healthy sugar metabolism. Why? As a result of generational patterns and lifestyle, our bodies do not have the enzymes to break down protein from non-meat sources, such as legumes or tofu, in order to extract and use the L-methionine. There is an exception—certain religious groups and cultures in India that are indigenously vegetarian have adapted over time to extract L-methionine from non-animal sources. Our bodies, over several more generations, probably will adapt. However, survival of the fittest, based on genetic adaptation and blood types, also are a factor. In the interim, we will continue to perpetuate a degenerative process in the body if we do not eat red meat. Tuna contains L-methionine. However, you would have to eat nine to twelve cans of tuna per day to get the same amount as you would get from nine ounces of red meat per week.

If L-methionine—the amino acid we get from eating red meat—is present, and we are eating it on a frequent basis, the communication between the liver, pancreas and adrenals is more efficient and better facilitated. That is the key to blood sugar metabolism—eating red meat to ensure that these pathways are turned on and in proper working order.

There is a lot of controversy about eating red meat. However, the controversy should not be about the *meat*, but rather the farming standards used in raising cows. According to a recent analysis by the Union of Concerned Scientists, 70 percent of the antibiotics produced in the United States each year, nearly 25 million pounds, are fed to *healthy* pigs, chickens and cattle to prevent disease or speed growth. The excessive use of antibiotics in livestock is contributing to the growing concerns about antibiotic resistance in humans. The majority of the red meat purchased in supermarkets contains massive amounts of antibiotics and hormones, unless the packaging specifies that the livestock have been organically raised without antibiotics or hormones. And if that isn't enough, most cows are grain fed, which is creating the same sugar metabolism imbalances we develop from eating grains.

The best meat is organic and grass-fed, free of antibiotics and hormones. Grass-fed meat has an optimal balance of essential fatty acids, which are important for many of the body's functions, including the immune system, hormonal balance and the nervous system.

Our brains are very specific about the nutrition they need in order to function. Our brains use glucose, the simplest form of sugar. There is something called the blood/brain barrier, a protective shield that protects the brain from toxicity. Glucose is the only nutrient that crosses the barrier into the brain. When we eat refined sugars and processed carbohydrates, the body breaks them down immediately, causing a spike in our blood sugar and a rush of insulin into our systems. It takes a lot of energy for the body to deal with this instant source of glucose. However, when we eat proteins or fats, the metabolic process is slower because not as much insulin is needed for digestion. The body maintains an even flow of glucose to the brain, rather than the spike reaction that occurs when we eat sugars or anything that breaks down like sugar, such as carbohydrates.

The key to creating that balance is controlling the eicosanoid reactions within the body. Eicosanoids are a hormone-like substance manufactured by every cell in the body. They are divided into Series 1 and Series 2:

Series 1	Series 2
Dilates blood vessels	Constricts blood vessels
Strengthens immune system	Weakens immune system
Reduces inflammation	Creates inflammation
Relieves pain	Increases pain
Increases oxygen	Decreases oxygen
Increases endurance	Decreases endurance
Prevents blood clotting	Promotes blood clotting
Dilates bronchial tubes	Constricts bronchial tubes
Fights cancer cell growth	Supports cancer cell growth

From: *The Sugar Control Bible and Cookbook*

The only way to control the balance of eicosanoid production is through food selection—choosing foods that are high in protein, low in carbohydrates and contain good fat. If you unlock a door with a key, whatever is inside that room is now at your disposal. When you eat sugar, the key opens the lock that secures the floodgates of insulin. When insulin is secreted, it causes a Series 2 eicosanoid reaction. On the other hand, when we eat protein such as eggs, steak, cheese, plain yogurt or raw cashews, the key unlocks a valve for glucagon, which unleashes a Series 1 eicosanoid reaction, enabling the body to heal.

It is important to eat protein frequently throughout the day and on a regular basis. Because protein is metabolized slowly, frequent eating will allow a consistent and even flow of glucose to the body. We are all aware that infants need to be fed every two hours. Even if we forget, the baby will let us know by crying or throwing a tantrum. As we age, our bodies let us know if we are not eating frequently enough. The message will come as fatigue, headache, concentration difficulties, irritability or bursts of anger. The LifeLine Technique enables the practitioner to assess the functional balance of sugar metabolism without the invasion of needles. Through the use of a kinesiological reflex and semantic testing, functional blood sugar metabolism and utilization can be assessed and balanced immediately.

This may surprise you, but blood sugar tests that require fasting are an ineffective way to assess blood sugar metabolism. The normal range of blood sugar is 80 to 120. Your blood sugar may get to 119 or 120, or it might go down to 80. The question is how quickly does it drop, and how quickly does it rise? Conducting the fasting blood glucose test every half hour ignores the fact that blood glucose can change within *five* minutes. If the test were conducted every 10 or 15 minutes, rather than 30, it could more easily be seen how quickly the blood sugar spikes, and an assessment would be more functional. Still, that is a pain. Who wants to be pricked with needles, drink a horrible sugar solution and feel terrible when it is very simple to do a muscle test? Muscle testing has been conducted effectively on hundreds of thousands of people throughout the world. It works.

Blood glucose numbers are not the only issue. What is critical is the body's adaptogenic property, its ability to return to balance. Whether the blood glucose is too high, too low or both, it is just a matter of turning the system back on so that it can maintain its own balance. The traditional paradigm of blood glucose treatment determines whether it is too high (diabetes) or too low (hypoglycemia) and medicates accordingly. However, on any given day, your blood sugar can fluctuate high or low, depending on whether your system is maintaining balance. That balance is based on water consumption, eating habits, rest, exercise and how you manage stressful situations.

The essence of holistic and energy medicine is balance. It lets the body find *its* "normal," which is *different* for everyone. By eating six to eight small meals daily, by drinking water and eating high quality foods, your body will balance itself.

I recommend you use _The Sugar Control Bible and Cookbook_ by Dr. Jacqueline Paltis. The program emphasizes frequent eating, every two hours, and requires some form of protein at that time. In addition, the program recommends:

- ❏ Eating a minimum of nine ounces of red meat per week.
- ❏ Drinking a quart of water per fifty pounds of body weight or any fraction thereof. For example, a 153-pound person needs four quarts of water per day.
- ❏ Elimination of all sweeteners, natural and artificial.
- ❏ Elimination or severe restriction of caffeine and nicotine.

The Chicago area, where I practice, recently was designated as one of the most overweight cities in the country. Obesity has become a chronic disease in the United States and the second leading cause of preventable death. Like its successful "Smoke-Out" urging people to stop smoking, the American Cancer Society recently launched a "Great American Weigh-In" in an effort to increase awareness of the risks of obesity, which is about to edge out smoking as the nation's number one _preventable_ public health crisis.

Obesity is our nation's most neglected public health challenge, and I believe the greatest culprit is sugar addiction and internalized, denied and disconnected emotions. Unlike other high-protein programs, the primary goal of The Sugar Control Program is _health gain_ instead of weight loss, although loss of weight is a by-product. Rather than focusing on dieting and the latest diet craze, it is important that we shift our focus to improving the quality of our health by developing a lifestyle that nourishes the body, rather than one that destroys it.

Chapter Twenty-Four

Food: A Healthy Eating Program

Diet is a four-letter word, and the first three letters are d-i-e. That says a lot. Fad diets may result in quick weight loss, but ultimately they create a yo-yo cycle that often leads to dis-ease and/or illness. That is why The Five Basics for Optimal Health incorporate a *healthy eating program*, rather than a diet.

Carbohydrate metabolism imbalances and sub-clinical dehydration are the leading culprits behind most chronic, degenerative diseases. The eating guidelines contained in this book will help your body heal.

Before I outline the program, let me give you a few tips that I recommend to my patients. They will help you successfully integrate these healthful changes into your life. The more organized you are, the easier it will be to integrate healthful eating into your daily routine.

❑ Read Dr. Paltis's book before beginning the program. It will help you understand how the quantity, quality and frequency of your food choices affect your health.

❑ Follow the recipes in *The Sugar Control Bible*, or modify your favorite recipes using permitted foods.

❏ It is helpful to use a grocery list when you go shopping. You will more likely purchase foods on the program rather than foods that are not on the permitted list.

❏ Whenever possible, prepare your staple foods in advance at least twice a week—roasted rice, raw vegetables, cheese, hardboiled eggs, and plain yogurt with fresh fruit.

❏ Set the timer in your electronic organizer, your watch or your computer as a conscious reminder to eat every two hours. Keep a food log in a small notebook (or in your electronic organizer). Write down the time of your meal or snack as well as what you ate.

❏ Review your food log weekly to keep track of your progress.

❏ Note how you feel after each meal so that you become aware of any food sensitivities.

❏ If you find that you have to eat out or are invited to a dinner party, snack before you go. If you snack, it is easier to resist the temptation of bread or sweets on the table.

❏ Keep apples and a bag of cashews and/or Brazil nuts in your car in case of an emergency.

The Sugar Control Healthy Eating Program is based on meals of fresh vegetables and fruits; antibiotic- and hormone-free, grass-fed meats; dairy products; and a limited amount of sprouted grains. The following information outlines the foods permitted when following the Sugar Control Healthy Eating Program as well as the foods that should be avoided.

PERMITTED FOODS FOR HEALTHY EATING
(*ALL FOODS PREFERABLY ORGANIC*)

Fresh Fruits and Vegetables	Green vegetables—unlimited
	Yellow vegetables—no more than four to six servings per week
	Fruits—unlimited
	Juices—Freshly juiced vegetables are permitted (one cup/day). No fruit juices unless freshly juiced. Carrot juice is allowed in limited amounts.
Meat and Dairy Unlimited	Beef, venison or buffalo (*at least 9 oz. per week required*)
	Lamb—Poultry—Pork

	Liver or other organ meats
	Fish and shellfish
	Eggs
	Cheese and cottage cheese
	Whole milk (only if there is no allergy, skin condition or weight challenge)
	Yogurt—plain, whole milk
Protein Snacks	Raw cashews and Brazil nuts
	Yellow/white aged cheese
	Raw cashew butter (made at home)
	You must eat some protein every two hours of your waking day
Beverages	**Water—one quart for every 50 pounds of body weight, rounded up to the next quart**
	Coffee and tea can be consumed in quantities of 1–3 cups/day. Whole milk or cream may be added; *no sweeteners permitted.* (Drink one additional cup of water for every cup of coffee/tea consumed.) Although coffee is permitted on the Sugar Control Program, we recommend removing it from your diet because coffee leads to a cortisol release from your adrenal glands, which causes inflammatory reactions throughout the body. Also, coffee, even organic, contains carboxcylic acid, which can destroy the intestinal wall leading to a dysbiosis—a "leaky gut."
Whole Grains	**Roasted Whole Grain Rice—unlimited quantity.**
	Use any variety of whole grain rice.
	Wash the rice and then toast it in a dry skillet over low to medium heat for about 15 minutes, stirring as you go, until the rice is golden brown. If the kernels begin to crackle and pop, lower the heat. Cool and store or cook immediately. Bring liquid to boil (1 C. rice to 3 C. water). Cook covered over low heat for 45 minutes, stirring one or two times. Homemade broth may replace some or all of the water. Herbs may be used for flavor. You can have as much of this rice as you like. Toasting the whole grain rice first makes the body

	use the rice as a protein, instead of as a starch. Serve it hot as a side dish to replace starches. The toasted rice makes excellent fried rice (see recipes in Dr. Paltis's book). Eat any left-over plain rice in the morning, mixed with plain, whole milk yogurt and fruit. It makes a delicious and satisfying breakfast. (You can add cinnamon for extra flavor!)
Bread—Sprouted Grain Only	**100% sprouted grain bread, *no more than two slices per day*** You will find this bread in the freezer section of some health food stores and better grocery stores. My favorite brand is Food For Life's Ezekiel 4:9™ Sprouted Grain Bread. Food for Life also makes sprouted grain tortillas, hamburger and hot dog buns. Honey or sweeteners are okay as ingredients in this bread. Just read the label and *make sure that the grains are 100% sprouted.* There are many "sprouted grain breads" that contain **both** sprouted and unsprouted flour. They are to be avoided.
Miscellaneous	Vinegar, herbs, spices, mustard, Braggs Liquid Aminos, condiments Be a label reader; as long as a prepared food or condiment contains no sugar (or dextrose, sucrose, corn syrup or fructose), it is permitted. All commercial and health food mayonnaises contain either sugar or honey, and health food mayonnaise is made with canola oil. There's a great recipe for mayonnaise in *The Sugar Control Bible.*
Vegetable Oils	Olive, sesame, walnut, sunflower, safflower **(*avoid peanut oil and canola oil*) Cook only with olive oil or butter (ghee).**
All Sprouts	Bean sprouts, alfalfa sprouts, sprouted lentils, sprouted grains
Cooked wine	In prepared foods

PROHIBITED FOODS

The following foods are not permitted while you are following The Sugar Control Plan. Strictly avoid these foods during that time. Follow the plan for two to six weeks, by listening to your body or working with your LifeLine Practitioner. After that period, follow the 80/20 plan. Regaining a balanced blood sugar metabolism is the key to finding your way back to optimal health.

Sugar	White sugar, brown sugar, dextrose, malt, fructose, sucrose, corn syrup, rice syrup, etc.
Natural Sweeteners	Honey, stevia, sucanat, molasses, maple syrup, barley malt, MSG
Artificial Sweeteners	Aspartame, saccharin, sorbitol, Equal, Nutrasweet, Sweet & Low, Splenda
Wheat Products	Bread, pasta, cereal, crackers, etc.
Seeds	Pumpkin and sunflower, etc.
Grains	Barley, oats, corn, millet, spelt, amaranth, rye, etc.
White Rice	Rice crackers, rice cakes, rice syrup, rice milk, Rice Dream
Prohibited Vegetables	Cauliflower, parsnips, beets, rutabagas, all canned and frozen vegetables
Prohibited Fruit Items	Dried fruit, canned and frozen fruit, fruit juices, jelly, preserves or fruit spread (sugar added)
Potatoes	White potatoes, sweet potatoes, yams, potato chips, French fries
Sweets	Ice cream and frozen yogurt, cookies and cake, candy and chewing gum, carob
Beverages	Beer, wine, liquor, soda pop and tonic water
Nuts	Peanuts, peanut butter, roasted nut butters, pecans, walnuts, etc.
Soy	Soy milk, tofu
Legumes	Beans, lentils, peas, soy
Starch	Rice starch, potato starch, cornstarch
Cooking Spray	Any and all
Condiments	Ketchup or barbecue sauce, soy sauce, MSG, margarine

THE 80/20 EATING PLAN

The 80/20 Eating Plan should be employed after strictly following the Sugar Control Program for a minimal of two to six weeks. Eighty percent of the time you should follow this eating program 100 percent. For example:

❑ Make sure that you eat a serving of protein every two hours.

❑ Eat a minimum of nine ounces of red meat per week.

❑ Eat unlimited amounts of fresh green vegetables and fresh fruits.

❑ Avoid the prohibited foods previously listed.

The other 20 percent of the time, you should live life to the fullest. Life is to be celebrated. That means on holidays, vacations, anniversaries, birthdays or days that you declare to be special for you, have fun! Just be in tune with how you are feeling in the moment. If you are having a good time, it usually means your mind, body and spirit are in balance. Your body metabolizes the foods on the prohibited list more efficiently when you are feeling on top of your game. If for whatever reason you are not feeling balanced, make sure to strictly follow the program 100 percent to enable your body to heal from the physical or emotional challenges you are facing. Most people will eat sugary foods when they are under a lot of stress, but that is the time when your body needs to focus on the situation at hand rather than on foods that are difficult to digest and metabolize. Otherwise, enjoy a piece of birthday cake, have a glass of wine, sink your teeth into a baked potato, or even add some ketchup to your favorite hamburger. What is most important is that you do your best to follow the 80/20 Eating Plan and authentically live in the moment.

CHAPTER TWENTY-FIVE

Rest:
You Heal When You Sleep

There is a direct link between the quality of your sleep and the quality of your health. How well you rest is determined by whether you drink enough water, eat healthy foods, exercise daily and own your power.

Far too many people suffer from insomnia, which can have an emotional, bio-chemical, structural or spiritual root. Causes of insomnia include a diet too high in sugar and refined carbohydrates; dehydration; physical or emotional trauma or stress; and not getting enough exercise.

Sleep deprivation not only affects the body's immune system, it can speed up the aging process and the onset of metabolic or hormonal imbalances. According to an October 1999 issue of the British medical journal *Lancet*, chronic sleep loss can speed the onset of Type-2 diabetes, high blood pressure, obesity and memory loss. It also can affect your mental and emotional state. Ever wonder why children and many adults are cranky when they do not get enough rest? In addition to fatigue, some of the effects of lack of sleep include irritability, blurred vision, slurring of speech, short-term memory lapses, an inability to concentrate, and hallucinations. Keep in mind that the amount of rest you need is impacted by the state of your health, level of stress and your age.

The parasympathetic nervous system is the part of the nervous system activated for healing. When you are healing from an injury, illness or emotional trauma, or when you are depressed, it is quite common to feel fatigued. Your body is telling you that it needs more rest. When you are asleep, the parasympathetic nervous system is functioning at its highest level. This allows the body to slow down, regenerate, and focus on problematic areas. In other words, when you sleep, you heal.

Dreams increase during your body's healing/detoxification phase. They are a fantastic tool for understanding and facilitating your healing process. Since they are usually metaphorical rather than literal, it is helpful to write down your dreams as soon as you awaken. Using The LifeLine Technique, you can release the subconscious patterns of your dreams, which helps you gain clarity about their meaning, and, in turn, expedites the healing process.

Posture, quantity, as well as quality of rest all play a major role in your overall health. The healthiest posture for sleeping is on either side or your back. Use pillows to support the natural curves in your spine. A pillow under the knees, while lying on your back, will support the lumbar spine. A single pillow under your neck will support the natural curve in your cervical spine. Hugging a pillow or keeping one pillow under your head will help maintain proper alignment between your cervical spine and thoracic spine. Or, if you sleep on your side, it is best to keep a pillow between your knees in order to maintain proper alignment within your pelvis.

Proper posture is imperative for proper health of the spinal column. The same applies when you are sleeping. Sleeping on your stomach will result in the compression of nerves in your cervical and lumbar spine, and the flattening of your thoracic spine. Common symptoms associated with sleeping on your stomach include spinal misalignments, headaches, numbness in the arms and hands, as well as a number of other neuro-musculoskeletal challenges. Any posture held for an extended period of time—such as hunching over a computer keyboard or bending the neck to read—will impact your ability to sleep. These symptoms will be magnified if your posture already is poor.

When it comes to rest, there are a couple of things you should remember. On an average, you should get between seven and nine hours of sleep per night. Children need more. Because the quantity of sleep necessary is different for everyone, use muscle testing to discover the specific number of hours your body needs for optimal health.

Making sure you receive quality rest and relaxation is the most significant step you can take to reduce the stress of modern living so that you can live healthier and happier. Just as you prepare to start your day, you should also prepare for sleep. Follow these tips to get a good, restful night of sleep:

❑ Spend fifteen to thirty minutes winding down before going to bed by taking the time to be quiet, meditate, read, journal or listen to soft music.

❑ Perform deep breathing exercises to facilitate relaxation.

❑ Do not watch television right before you go to bed or fall asleep with it turned on.

❑ Eat a high-protein snack and a small piece of fruit several hours before you go to bed.

❑ Take a hot bath, shower or sauna before bed.

❑ To maximize your ability to get a good night's rest, avoid caffeine, medications (if possible) and alcohol just before you go to bed.

❑ Reserve your bed for sleeping, rather than using it as an alternative site for work.

The act of sleeping not only enables your body to heal, it also enables your mind to process and integrate your life experiences. Sleep is a wonderful tool to increase the potential of the body's natural healing capacity, especially when you are overwhelmed by stress. In many countries throughout the world it is commonplace to have a time of day where everyone takes a nap. Make time to take a fifteen minute siesta and give your body and mind the ability to regenerate and relax.

CHAPTER TWENTY-SIX

Creating A New Vision for Your Life

We breathe in order to bring oxygen into the body in a cycle that nourishes the body and purifies the blood. How we breathe is very important in determining how we feel and how we think. For example, when we are sad or anxious, we breathe in short gasps. Normal, unconscious breathing is controlled through the autonomic nervous system. Focused breathing is an act of self-awareness, an act of staying in the moment and a reminder that we are alive. By switching the breathing to a conscious, controlled action, you form a link between the conscious mind, deeper emotional states and spiritual fulfillment.

Take a moment to pay attention to your breath. Breathe as you normally do. Most likely your chest rises and falls. Become aware of your chest and the muscles that move. Repeat this breathing a few times. Remember this feeling. This is shallow breathing. You may have noticed that if you breathe hard this way for long periods, your chest begins to hurt.

The breath is the vehicle through which you maintain Present Time Consciousness. It is the link between the mind, the body and the spirit, and when you are in tune with your breathing you are connected to your spirit.

In Yoga, the asanas (postures) are a great way to prepare the body to sit for pranayama (breathing exercises) and meditation. The main focus of attention should be on the connection between the breath and the movement of the spine. The focus of the *inhale* is on the expansion of the upper chest, rib cage and abdominal areas creating extension of the spine and flattening of the upper back. The focus of the *exhale* is on the contraction of the abdominal muscles from the pubic bone to navel, stabilizing the pelvis to help flatten the curve in the low back.

The following breathing exercises were recommended by my Yoga instructor, Erin Walsh Rodriguez. Create time to either start or finish your day with these breathing exercises:

UJJAYI BREATH

In Ujjayi breath, there is a slight contraction in the back of the throat (at the glottis) that makes a whisper-like sound. Start by making an *"hhhaaaaa"* sound as you exhale, first with the mouth open, and then close it halfway through the breath as you continue to exhale. Then keep the mouth closed as you inhale and exhale, listening for the whisper-like sound. Cover your ears with the palm of your hands to internalize the sound. This is a heating breathing technique.

a) Focus on the inhale and exhale equally.

b) Focus on the inhalation, gradually lengthening it (i.e., start with a four-second inhale, then progress to five seconds, six, seven, eight, etc.). Let the exhalation be free (no counting but equal to or longer than the inhale.) This has an energizing, stimulating effect.

c) Focus on the exhalation, progressively lengthening the exhalation (same as previous), letting the inhalation be free (no counting). This has a calming, grounding effect.

d) After the breathing, sit and feel the effects.

RATIO

There are four parts to the breath: The inhale, the pause after the inhale called retention, the exhale and the pause after the exhale, which is called suspension. Working with retention and suspension adds a deeper dimension to the breath. Samavrtti means "same" so the inhale, exhale, retention and suspension are equal.

a) Be aware of the four parts of the breath.

b) Bring the inhale and exhale to an equal count, and the pauses (retention and suspension) to an equal count (e.g., inhale eight seconds, pause for two seconds, exhale eight seconds and pause for two seconds. That is one round.)

c) Samavrtti. The inhale, retention, exhale, suspension are all equal (e.g., inhale six seconds, retain six seconds, exhale six seconds, suspend six seconds.) This is quite advanced.

Guidelines: *Never* force the breath. The exhalation is always equal to or longer than the inhalation. The exhalation is always equal to or longer than the retention (hold after inhalation). Let the focus be on the smooth flow of the breath.

Do at least twelve rounds of breathing. After the pranayama technique of your choice, sit and feel the effects physically in the spine, hips and legs and in the capacity of the lungs. Feel the effects emotionally—do you feel stable, nurtured, calm? Feel the effects mentally through clarity of mind and focus. Feel the effects spiritually—do you feel connected to something higher? Also, notice any feelings of discomfort, instability, irritability, confusion, disconnection, and use The Life-Line Technique to find out what is causing these feelings.

Even if it is only ten minutes each day, giving yourself time alone creates awareness that your mind is always filled with thoughts. Taking time to be aware of those thoughts, to accept them while continuing to breathe, is a way to reconnect with your inner self. I like to visualize a flame inside my mind. The more thoughts I have, the brighter the flame flickers. As I let the thoughts float through me, I enter a space described by Deepak Chopra as the "space between thoughts."

When you get to that place, the flame is bright and fills the mind. Achieving solitude in the "space between your thoughts" opens the window to your feelings. It helps you develop a deeper awareness of who you are and the unlimited potential you possess. It is the moment in which you are *be-ing*, rather than *do-ing*; it is the "being" part of your humanness, which Ram Dass defined as "be here now." We are called human beings, instead of human do-ers, because we need to *be*. Just to sit and just to be.

Visualization combined with focused breathing is another way to harness your energy. The integration between visualization and the focused breathing will help you understand and know the "right now." While "right now" is different for everyone, every moment is an opportunity to know your truth and refill your spirit with passion, excitement and joy.

Use the following exercises to explore the effects of visualization and focused breathing:

VISUALIZE YOUR LIGHT

Using Ujjayi breathing, you can visualize by simply lighting a candle and sitting comfortably on the floor or in a chair. If you like, use very gentle, instrumental music and incense. Breathe gently and deeply by slowly inhaling through your nose and exhaling through your mouth. Focus your breath. Let your mind flow and pay attention to whatever color emerges. Now, with each inhale, visualize this color as a beam of light that starts at your toes and moves up and through your body. The goal is to focus your mind on this beam of light and to control its ascent as you breathe more and more deeply, filling your body with light.

CREATING A MAGICAL HAVEN

Using Ujjayi breathing, gradually allow your mind to enter a place, real or imagined, that is quite special to you. Let your mind drift to this pleasant, peaceful haven. It is a place that you know, one where you always can relax completely because you feel secure and safe. It is a place where no one or nothing can bother you. It can be a room, a house in the country or a beach. It is your magical haven. Now imagine this place in detail. Notice the light. Is it bright or dim, natural or man-made? Is it hot, warm or cool? What is the source of heat? What are the colors, sounds, smells that surround you? The shapes and textures? Are there any familiar objects that make this place special? Breathe in and out slowly, relaxing more deeply in your magical haven.

BALANCING STRESS WITH INFINITE LOVE & GRATITUDE

Take some time to focus on a stressful experience in your life. As you begin to zoom in on this picture and see it more clearly, pay attention to the emotions that are evoked within you. With your intention, send that part of you Infinite Love & Gratitude. Now, be in tune with the thoughts, images or memories that emerge as your mind focuses on the stressful situation. As you do, send these thoughts, images and memories Infinite Love & Gratitude. Now, focus on your body and pay attention to how it feels to focus on the stressful situation. Does your body feel heavy or tight? How does your breath feel? Is your balance affected in any way? Whatever feelings arise within your body, send Infinite Love & Gratitude to that part of your body and to that feeling. Now, focus your attention on the voice inside of your mind as you focus on the stressful situation. Pay attention to the beliefs that you have about yourself in this stressful situation. Send Infinite Love & Gratitude to those beliefs. After you finish this exercise, pay attention to how it feels to focus on the stressful situation. You will notice that you no longer have a negative charge towards the stressful experience.

With visualization we can proactively use The LifeLine Law of Transformation and Creation to create the life we desire. Our *emotions transform energy; energy creates movement; movement creates change; and change is the essence of life.* When we utilize positive visualization, we transform energy into an attractor field of success, inner peace and health.

Remember Arlene, the woman discussed at the beginning of the book who had been diagnosed with macular degeneration? As part of taking responsibility for her health, she used positive visualization to enhance her body's ability to heal. Through visualization and deep breathing, Arlene imagined her eyes 100 percent healed. She consistently thought the words, "Infinite Love & Gratitude," as she focused on her eyes. She acknowledged the feelings of anger that she had internalized, denied and disconnected from and used visualization to transform that anger into appreciation for her experience and what she learned as a result. Arlene released the limiting belief she had about the macular degeneration being permanent. Prior to seeing her ophthalmologist, she was already aware that her eyes had healed. Her doctor just reconfirmed what she had already visualized within her mind.

You must imagine yourself healthy or having already overcome the challenge in order to succeed. Take the time daily to visualize challenging situations. Visualize the successful resolution in your mind and then observe its creation in your life. By taking the time to visualize a positive resolution while being present with your breath, you are focusing your intention on creating a new vision for your life. Positive thoughts and focused breathing transform the energy of any challenging situation, thus enabling you to move in your desired direction.

CHAPTER TWENTY-SEVEN

Living Life One Moment at a Time

Do you ever feel drained because your intention, focus and energy are pulling you in multiple directions? Does it affect your ability to accomplish even the simplest tasks? Why does this happen? When you are not connected to Present Time Consciousness, or PTC, you are as focused as diffused light.

PTC opens the mind and heart to truly experience a moment. It is that subtle awareness between comfort and discomfort. For example, while shaking hands, how tightly do you squeeze? Or while walking, are you aware of your posture? The subtle awareness that is gained by living in PTC provides you with the opportunity to make the appropriate adaptations that allow for the most optimal flow possible.

While sailing, it is imperative to be in touch with the wind. Let it guide you from moment to moment. When the wind picks up, pull in your sail and go for it. When the wind loses her power, loosen your hold on the sail and be patient. This will enable you to flow effortlessly. This is PTC.

Nature is a beautiful example of PTC. Nature follows the law of least effort. A tree does not expend any more energy than it needs to when the wind blows. In fact, the tree has specific enzymes that are secreted every time the winds blow that helps it to adapt to the stress of the wind. You also have enzymes and hormones that are secreted when you are under stress. Just as the tree, you become stronger with every challenging situation that you endure. However, when you do not practice PTC, you lose your ability to adapt and are at risk for injury and breakdown.

Every single moment provides you with an opportunity to maintain Present Time Consciousness. PTC is staying connected to your senses—what you see, hear, smell, feel, taste and how your intuition is guiding you in the moment. The more you are aware, the more you feel, think and react on the subtlest of levels. That is PTC.

A poem that beautifully expresses the potential we all have when living in PTC is called "Autobiography in Five Short Chapters." It was written by the late author and actress, Portia Nelson:

I.

I walk down the street.

There is a deep hole in the sidewalk.

I fall in.

I am lost . . . . I am helpless.

It isn't my fault.

It takes me forever to find a way out.

II.

I walk down the same street.

There is a deep hole in the sidewalk.

I pretend I don't see it.

I fall in again.

I can't believe I am in the same place.

But, it isn't my fault.

It still takes a long time to get out.

III.

I walk down the same street.

There is a deep hole in the sidewalk.

I see it is there.

I still fall in . . . . it's a habit.

My eyes are open.

I know where I am.

It is my fault.

I get out immediately.

IV.

I walk down the same street.

There is a deep hole in the sidewalk.

I walk around it.

V.

I walk down another street.

Knowing what you need and when you need it is the essence of PTC. When you are focusing on things of the past, when you are worried about the future, the worry gets in the way of living in the moment.

I had a patient named Gary whose chief complaint was abdominal pain whenever he walked. He could not walk twenty feet without feeling pain. Gary had a history of severe cardiovascular disease and had been given multiple prescription medications to alleviate the symptoms. Instead of getting better, the symptoms became worse. By the time Gary came to see me for treatment, he and his family were desperate.

During the initial evaluation, I took an x-ray of his spine. I was looking to see whether there was some aspect of referral pain radiating from his spine. I discovered that his abdominal aorta had completely calcified. Whenever Gary walked, the increase in blood flow caused the calcified arteries to expand beyond capacity. The result was intense pain. Gary was severely dehydrated and had a profound imbalance in his blood sugar metabolism. I used The LifeLine Technique to harmonize his body to the medications he was taking and had a discussion with his cardiologist about what I found.

During Gary's third visit, our work with The LifeLine Flow Chart revealed that he was internalizing feelings of grief that were causing a decreased flow of life force through his lung meridian. Gary told me he was mourning the death of his wife. I realized his internalized grief was at the root of why Gary was experiencing such extreme abdominal pain. I told him that it was imperative that he stay connected to his feelings of grief. I expressed to Gary that the tears he shed were a tribute to the love he had for his wife and the beautiful impact she had on his life.

Gary owned his power by confronting the challenge of grief, expressing his feelings whenever he experienced them. A month later, he began to notice that the abdominal pain was decreasing and even disappearing for much longer periods of time than ever before. During a follow up visit, Gary reported that for the first time in more than a year, he had been pain-free for five days. When there was pain, its severity had tremendously decreased. Gary continues to take supportive nutritional supplements and drainage formulas to help his body heal and observes The Five Basics for Optimal Health to support and facilitate the healing changes within his body.

Life can be challenging, and at times we feel as if there is no hope. What an honor and gift to help this beautiful man realize the inherent power he possesses as a human being. By learning to express his feelings and live in PTC, he profoundly changed his own life.

When you stay in the moment and focus on what is at hand, you not only feel more fulfilled, but you preserve and enhance your body's unlimited potential for healing.

While working on this book, there were times when I felt very focused and rooted in PTC. All of a sudden, the moment would disappear. What pulled me out of the moment? Without warning, I would be filled with doubt about whether I could clearly communicate what I needed to share as a holistic physician and teacher. Whatever the genesis of the insecurities I was feeling, staying in the moment clarified the lesson I needed to learn and allowed me to manifest my authentic self to write this book.

Uncomfortable emotions often times cause us to disconnect from PTC. Instead of experiencing pain, fear or challenges as an opportunity, we run, hide and numb ourselves. By staying connected to the pain, fear and challenges of life, we are able to learn from the experience and move on.

Denying pain or discomfort does not make it go away. It just escalates the damage and turns a painful moment into suffering. The body is more susceptible to breaking down when we disconnect from it. Imagine you are driving your car and your brake light starts blinking red, warning you of a potential hazard. Would you ever go into your glove compartment, pull out a hammer and smash the brake light, then continue driving as if nothing ever happened? That would be pretty silly because soon the brakes would fail, with or without the warning.

Think of a challenging situation and imagine your conscious awareness of that situation as a continuously flowing river. Observe how your emotions about the situation simultaneously pull you in a myriad of directions. Notice how it is much more difficult to deal with the situation when you are at the mercy of the river's current. Now, imagine stepping onto the river's bank. You will begin to appreciate the experience from an entirely new perspective. Pay attention to the emotions that have surfaced. From this vantage point, you are able to own your power and make a clearer, more rational decision about the situation. When you are in PTC, you are aware of your senses and emotions and have the ability to act or react authentically.

To the observer, the fight movements of martial artists seem to be moving at warp speed. But to the martial artist engaged in the fight, they occur in slow motion. These warriors are so used to being in PTC that every punch, every block, every movement, every flinch is split into "nano" pieces. In PTC, movement becomes the law of least effort, which was a motto of the extraordinary martial artist, the late Bruce Lee. Lee was able to break bricks and boards only one inch away from his hand. He could throw a person across the room with a one-inch punch because he used the least amount of effort within that one concentrated moment. Was it because he was super strong? No. Bruce Lee was the master of PTC.

It is your God-given right to have unlimited joy, love and passion, and if it is not happening, you have the power to make it happen. Right now is the time. It is not at the *end* of the journey; it *is* the journey itself. You do not have to wait until you make a million dollars, meet Mr./Ms. Right person, obtain the "perfect" body weight, or live in your dream house. None of these things change who you are on the inside. The only thing that changes what you feel inside is PTC—this is the right time to work on your life.

By learning about the basics of a healthy lifestyle—the quantity, quality and frequency of your water, food, rest, exercise and owning your power—you will take responsibility for your life and make the changes your life is telling you are necessary. Everyone has their own PTC. No one can tell you when or how to begin. The time is always right now.

CHAPTER TWENTY-EIGHT

Exercising Your Passion

Most of us are obsessed with our weight instead of being focused on our health. We believe we could be "fit and fabulous" if only there were a supplement or pill to take, instead of exercising and healthfully eating. Unfortunately, despite the millions of dollars earned by the makers of lose-weight-quick supplements, there is not a single product on the market that has been found to be the silver bullet—the product that turns an obese body into a *healthy* body. Some of them are even dangerous. The only way to become truly healthy is by embracing The Five Basics for Optimal Health.

Fitness is multifaceted, so you need a program that addresses this issue from all angles. Give yourself the gift of exercise every day, and it will dramatically change and add years to your life. Recent studies have shown that sixty minutes of daily exercise improves your body's ability to use insulin and metabolize food; helps you maintain a healthy weight; increases your energy levels and your mental clarity; contributes to healthy bones, muscles and joints; makes you stronger; improves your balance; reduces feelings of depression and anxiety; and heightens your self-esteem. If you do not have sixty minutes to spare, you can begin with fifteen.

This simple breathing exercise has no physical or age restrictions; anyone can do it. Lie on your back or sit in a chair. Focus on contracting and relaxing each part of your body. While maintaining a rhythmic, diaphragmatic breathing pattern, hold each contraction for ten seconds, and then relax for ten seconds. Begin with your feet by contracting and relaxing them. Next contract and relax your legs. Continue this process of contracting for ten seconds and then relaxing for ten seconds as you move up to your buttocks, low back, abdomen, chest, shoulders, arms, hands and then face. Finally, contract all the muscles of your entire body for five seconds and then relax your whole body for five seconds. Continue this exercise for a total of fifteen minutes. Feel the stress that you hold in your body just melt away. This exercise is a great way to jump start your day. It will enhance your circulation, lymphatic drainage and increase your vitality.

Beyond this, depending upon what your goals are, adding walking, weight training, cardiovascular training, Pilates or NIA (Neuromusclear Integrative Action) will help you build confidence, become stronger, more flexible and have endurance, both physically and mentally. Two of my favorite forms of exercise are Tai Chi and Qigong.

Tai Chi is the ancient Chinese art of moving meditation based on the Taoist understanding that all things comprise the harmony of two complementary forces, yin and yang. Through the study and practice of Tai Chi, you learn to apply the principles of yielding to overcome the unyielding and of the soft overcoming the hard. As the body learns to soften and yield through Tai Chi practice, the mind becomes more open and flexible, allowing you to focus your attention in a spontaneous manner and to have a deeper connection with the moment.

My Tai Chi Master utilizes Tai Chi exercise, meditation and application to help his students gain awareness of the infinite power of *chi*. I am in awe of his wisdom, power and gentle way of living. He explains: "Every experience is an opportunity to flow or be stuck. Use Tai Chi practices and meditations and apply them to the challenges you face in life."

Qigong is used for healing and increasing vitality. It is an integration of physical postures, breathing techniques and focused intention. The effect of both ancient arts is the reconnection of the mind and body to the spirit.

Do this Qigong exercise, *Stand Like A Tree*:

❏ Stand with your feet apart, about hip-width. Stack your spine on top of your hips, imagining a string of pearls stacking one on top of the other. Verify your alignment in front of a mirror. Rest your head at the center of the gravity that runs through your spine. Drop your chin and free the back of your neck. You may notice that you feel like falling forward, but you will not. Make sure your palms are parallel to the ground.

❑ As you stand, breathe deeply, expanding your stomach as you inhale, pulling your navel to your spine as you exhale. The goal is to connect to an open state of awareness while doing nothing else. Do this for one minute and work on extending the time to ten minutes. This may sound simple, but it can be extremely challenging at first. In the beginning, after just a few seconds you will begin to feel the resistance—blockages and stagnation—in your body. Your mind will become very noisy. Embrace the discomfort. It allows you to become acutely aware of what is going on in your mind and body and to expand your ability to use PTC. This will help heal your body at a much quicker rate. The longer you hold the tree posture, the more grounded and stronger your mind-body-spirit connection.

There are several key factors that are very important if you want to get the most benefit from exercise. First and foremost, each exercise program depends upon the individual. Your exercise program should be customized for your individual structural, emotional, biochemical, and spiritual needs. Seek out the assistance of a trained, licensed and certified professional in order to create a program that best suits you.

Make exercise one of your passions. The beauty about passion is that it evolves. Continue to explore new ways of strengthening your mind and body through your daily exercise program. Remember, it takes a minimal of nineteen days for a change in behavior to become a habit. Here are some steps you can take to develop the healthy habit of fitness:

❑ Set goals and write them down—the amount of time you will exercise and the types of exercise you will perform on which day.

❑ Every single day, mentally commit yourself to achieving your minimum of fifteen minutes of exercise. Dr. Lucia Capacchione, author of *Lighten Up Your Body—Lighten Your Life*, says the key to any lasting change is "to experience your body *as it is*." She recommends a relaxation and meditation exercise in which you take an inner journey through your body. The goal is to get to know your body, become sensitive to its changes and feel at home so that you are aware when physical and emotional changes take place.

❑ Stay in PTC while exercising. Stay in touch with your breathing and your body. The saying, "no pain, no gain," will get you in trouble. If any exercise is causing pain, stop. Your body is sending a warning signal to slow down.

❑ Reward yourself. Celebrate the fact that you are taking such good care of yourself.

❑ If you are having a hard time exercising by yourself, give the gift of exercise to a family member or friend by asking them to join you.

Exercise is one of the most crucial components of healing. Research has found that *everyone* can benefit from regular physical activity; even physical decline associated with aging can be *reversed* through exercise.

When was the last time you rode a bike? Went on a hike? Put on a pair of roller blades or ice skates? Danced? When was the last time you went for a walk that was not in a parking lot or a grocery store? One session of aerobic exercise has been found to help people with diabetes drop their blood glucose levels by as much as fifty to seventy points. Just imagine what a regular regime of exercise, combined with the other healthy lifestyle components, will do for your health and vitality!

There is an old adage: "What the mind conceives and believes it will achieve." Use the power of Infinite Love & Gratitude and The LifeLine Technique to release limiting beliefs, attitudes, self-destructive behaviors and addictions that are preventing you from achieving your health and fitness goals.

CHAPTER TWENTY-NINE

Own Your Power: Reclaiming Your Authentic Self

There is so much pain in life; pain that takes the form of fear, death, failure and shame. Without question, there will be times when life is overwhelming and you may not feel equipped to handle the pain. It is important to remember that you were not put on this magnificent planet to suffer. You are here to learn and awaken to the infinite potential that exists within you.

Owning your power is living life with Infinite Love & Gratitude. It means to embrace all aspects of life with passion, purpose and courage. Owning your power— reconnecting to the emotions that lie dormant in your subconscious mind—is the key to reclaiming your authentic self.

Over the past several years, many books have been written about the "authentic self." Webster's defines the word "authentic" as meaning *genuine* and *real*. Authenticity is different for everyone. It is being true to yourself in a way that only you know, because you can *feel* it—it feels easy, harmonious and congruent within. The same holds true when you are not being authentic with yourself; you get that uncomfortable feeling inside. It feels heavy somewhere in your body. You also know when people are not being authentic with you. It is a gut reaction that you feel immediately.

No matter what situation you are experiencing, it is vital to view it through the authenticity of your heart. Your heart speaks without judgment. Your emotions are a pure reflection of what you are experiencing. By embracing life with an open heart, your authentic self, you are able to transform chaos into harmony. It is said, "Life isn't about finding yourself. Life is about creating yourself." By choosing to own your power, embracing the moment, the burdens of your past will no longer hinder you from seeing your future.

Many of us have a long history of being disconnected from our emotions, dating back to childhood. Our parents, as a result of their own disconnections, warned us against expressing our emotions. They often said: "You should be seen but not heard," or "Be a big boy/girl, don't cry." Consequently, we were not encouraged to express our emotions and feelings associated with the experiences.

The best way to reconnect to your feelings is to pay attention to what your body is telling you. Remember, your body speaks with symptoms that are the result of emotions being triggered in the subconscious mind. Every feeling and resulting emotion is the body talking loud and clear. Notice, for example, that when you find someone difficult to deal with, that person literally becomes a "pain in the neck." Or think about the times when you have a "gut reaction" to a person or an event. Denying your intuitive feelings causes the body to speak. The longer you internalize your feelings, the louder your body will yell.

If you have an uncomfortable feeling, but you are unable to immediately pinpoint it, take some time to be still and quiet. Focus on your body and scan it. Of what sensations are you aware? What emotions emerge? After you have pinpointed the feelings, the next step is to own your power and authentically express your feelings.

In terms of health, the *real* self is the person who speaks his or her mind, shares feelings, expresses emotion and feels comfortable saying no when it is appropriate. For most of us, expressing feelings and emotions is difficult.

The word "emotion" can be broken down into two parts: "e" and "motion." "E" stands for energy, and "motion" means movement, which means *all emotions must stay in motion*. When you repress your emotions internally and do not express them authentically, it forces your body to find another language to release them. This body language can be a pain, an organ dysfunction, imbalanced sugar metabolism or numerous other symptoms associated with the mind-body-spirit connection. Open expression of emotion—owning your power—is a key component of healing. There is scientific research to substantiate this.

Dr. Candace Pert, researcher, neurobiologist and author of *Molecules of Emotion*, has demonstrated the connection between our emotions and our health. She discovered neuropeptides, which are the chemicals in the body triggered by emotions:

> *My research has shown me that when emotions are expressed—which is to say that the biochemicals that are the substrate of emotion are flowing freely—all systems are united and made whole. When emotions are repressed, denied, not allowed to be whatever they may be, our network pathways get blocked, stopping the flow of the vital feel-good, unifying chemicals that run both our biology and behavior.*

The LifeLine Flow Chart guides us through the emotional maze of the Five Elements, demonstrating how life force or *chi* becomes blocked within the acupuncture meridians of the body. Grief, for example, is associated with the metal element and travels in the lung/large intestine acupuncture meridian. Fear is associated with the water element and travels in the bladder-kidney acupuncture meridian. When we internalize, deny or disconnect from an emotion, it leads to a decreased flow of our life force through the acupuncture meridians. For example, internalized grief can cause the body to respond with the symptoms of sinus blockages or bronchitis. The decreased flow in our life force triggers our bodies to speak with symptoms. When we ignore symptoms—the voice of the body—it leads to pathology or a complete breakdown in the body.

According to ancient Buddhist teachings, change is a process of opening, learning and training the mind. Most of us have learned to disconnect from pain. This denial of pain prevents authentic healing from occurring. However, by embracing the pain we are able to let go of it, therefore facilitating healing on its deepest levels. Just as a wound needs to be cleaned of dirt and debris so it will heal, internalized emotions also need to be released. The LifeLine Technique removes the true causes of symptoms and disease, thereby helping you to feel. *Remember, you must learn to feel if you want to heal.*

I have a friend who lives in Europe. In the spring, she sent me an e-mail about the breakthrough she had with allergies:

> *I figured out that most of the allergies were psychological. I was having a "wild" relationship at that time, and anytime anything went wrong, it was hard for me*

to breathe. I was unable to figure out what the problem was. There did not seem to be a specific allergy component. As soon as I got out of the relationship, the symptoms began to improve.

The asthma symptoms my friend was experiencing went away.

A commonly experienced emotion is anger, which generally is a result of hurt. Hurt is a by-product of feelings denied and minds not spoken in the first place—it is a cycle of pain that only you have the power to break. Unexpressed anger causes a decreased flow in the liver/gall bladder acupuncture meridians, resulting in the body having a difficult time detoxifying poisons and toxins.

I had a patient with breast cancer. When we began to work together, she was making amazing strides, and her oncologist was extremely happy about the way she was healing. Everything seemed to be progressing well. One day she told me that she believed she developed cancer so that her husband would pay attention to her and treat her with more respect. Well, her husband did pay more attention to her and treat her with greater respect once she received the diagnosis. But as soon as she began to heal, he went back to his old ways. Lo and behold, the cancer began to spread. She told me she "hated him"; however, she was afraid of hurting his feelings and upsetting her children. She chose not to speak her truth and she died a short while later.

The chemicals the body produces with anger are so extremely toxic that, left internalized, they will fester into disease. Unless anger is expressed, the body will not heal.

Dr. Deepak Chopra says, "There is no purpose in suffering except as a guide to your truth." In other words, pain can provide a road map to reclaiming your authentic self, but to follow the map you have to acknowledge and release the pain as soon as it occurs. You have to pay attention to your feelings. Stay in Present Time Consciousness and speak your truth!

You can reconnect with your feelings through:

❏ Exercise
❏ Meditation
❏ Maintaining Present Time Consciousness
❏ Journaling
❏ Writing poetry, stories or songs
❏ Listening to yourself and listening to others

❑ Forgiveness
❑ Music
❑ Dancing
❑ Painting
❑ Any aspect of creative expression
❑ Treatments with The LifeLine Technique

One of the great benefits of The LifeLine Flow Chart is that it helps us pinpoint where and how we have internalized, denied or disconnected from our emotions. It points to the effect this disconnection, internalization or denial is having on us, and releases it from the subconscious mind.

With The LifeLine treatments, you begin to witness and experience the connection between your feelings and the pain or dysfunction in your body. You soon develop a deeper sense of awareness about yourself and your environment; you learn to trust your intuition and feelings. You begin to *create* authenticity for yourself. In other words, you respond when your body speaks with a symptom, telling you that you are not being true to yourself. The beautiful thing about this process is that there is no such thing as failure. Life will continuously challenge you, creating situations to test how authentic you are. Each moment will push, lead, pull, drag or block your way to the next moment. And you will *feel* that motion somewhere in your body. The more you practice owning your power, the better you will be at moving with the flow of life.

CHAPTER THIRTY

Children: The Bridge to the Future

Childhood is a sacred time, a time of wonder, innocence and authenticity. Children hungrily and attentively see, touch, taste, hear, feel, seek, reach and pull, absorbing the world around them through all of their senses. They are unabashed about expressing their feelings. When they are happy and joyful, children smile, giggle or laugh. When they are upset, they yell, scream or cry. The beauty of a child's spirit is his or her ability to live in PTC and to be authentic in the moment.

As children mature, they begin to learn patterns of self-expression based on interactions with their families, neighbors, teachers, religious leaders and other adults in their environment. Children imprint and mirror their environment; they are a reflection of the internalized or denied thoughts, feelings and beliefs of their parents. Therefore, there is a subtle but necessary balance between guiding, protecting and parenting children and inhibiting them with the fears and taboos of family, society, race, religion, or the planet. That is why it is so important that parents maintain PTC in all of their interactions with their children. Raising a child is conscious behavior, just as love is a learned behavior, and people who accept the responsibility for molding and shaping another human being's life must do so with conscientious and loving care.

How? Teach your children to own their power, to believe in themselves, to be optimistic and to believe in the infinite power and capacity that we all have as human beings to love, to heal, to succeed and to achieve any goals we are willing to work hard enough to make happen. Most important, give your children the gift of health by introducing them to The LifeLine Technique treatments and philosophy. Help them to maintain The Five Basics for Optimal Health—quantity, quality and frequency of water, food, rest, exercise and owning their power.

According to the World Health Organization (WHO), the American Academy of Pediatrics (AAP) and the journal *Pediatrics,* today's children are suffering the ravaging effects of a nutrient-poor diet based on junk food, soda, caffeine and sugar, as well as the effects of watching too much television. The results: Obesity, tooth decay, allergies, asthma, nervous system disorders, depression, anxiety, lethargy, learning disabilities, sensory integration difficulties, social skills dysfunction, hyperactivity and violent behavior are at crisis levels among children. The allopathic medical community's response is to say these children suffer from Attention Deficit Disorder (ADD) and Attention Deficit Hyperactive Disorder (ADHD), and to prescribe stimulants and antidepressants, as well as a slew of other drugs, for every symptom they encounter.

Dr. Fred Baughman, Jr., who has more than thirty-five years of experience as a neurologist and pediatric neurologist, is one of the nation's most vocal opponents of the use of pharmacological drugs to deal with ADHD. He says the drugging of millions of normal children is "the single, biggest health care fraud in the U.S." According to Dr. Baughman, a half-million children were diagnosed with ADHD in 1985. Today, the WHO assails the "dangerous proportions" of children on drugs to be between five and seven million.

A recent study by the University of Michigan, published by *Pediatric Academic Societies* in May of 2000, found that the latest trend among physicians is to prescribe both stimulant drugs *and* antidepressants at the same time. The lead author of the study, himself a medical doctor, said: "One of the biggest questions this study raises is whether the children who are prescribed both types of medication have both types of disorders, or whether their physicians are recommending these medications for other reasons."

I have successfully treated thousands of children who have been diagnosed with ADD and ADHD, conditions that are a result of many factors, including blood sugar metabolism imbalances, dehydration, overexposure to electromagnetic energy from computers and television, overmedication, lack of communication within the family, and the yearning of the child for attention.

Alec, a nine-year-old patient, was diagnosed with ADD. His teacher was putting pressure on his parents to have him placed on medication, but Alec's parents were resistant and looking for a healthier route than taking pills to control his behavior. They realized that there must be more to his behavioral challenges; after all, Alec had exhibited the ability to follow instructions and excel in the martial arts. Did he have ADD or was something else going on?

Fortunately, Alec's mother—already a patient—decided to bring him in for an evaluation. Through The LifeLine Technique, I found that Alec had a major sugar metabolism imbalance and was sensitive to wheat and dairy foods. We balanced his blood sugar by changing his eating program and harmonized him to the allergies. Within a few weeks, Alec had made great strides at home and at school. His teachers and mother have noticed enormous improvements in his behavior and health. Aware now of foods that impact his health in a negative way, Alec is making much wiser choices and feeling better about himself.

Jake, a seven-year-old, had been prescribed five medications—Lithium, Adderall, Celexa, Clonidine and Strattera. His mother contacted me because Jake was having trouble with constipation, which she believed was the cause of his difficulties. She thought that Jake's behavioral challenges were a result of the poisons and toxins trapped in his body due to the constipation.

Using The LifeLine Technique, I harmonized Jake to the medications that he was taking because I knew that they were harming him. However, as I have said earlier, it is not within my licensure to recommend that someone stop taking medication. It is important that the doctor who prescribed the medications be the one to wean the child. Going off medications too quickly can be disastrous.

Jake's parents took responsibility and helped their son to understand and follow The Five Basics for Optimal Health. Within a month, there were major improvements in Jake's attitude, health and behavior. His bowels began moving multiple times a day, and there was a dramatic change in his self-esteem. Unfortunately, Jake's medical doctor was initially resistant to weaning the boy off the medications. However, his parents have owned their power and have been insistent. As I write this book, Jake now only takes one of the five medications, and the process of weaning him off the last medication is about to begin.

How can we possibly justify giving stimulants and anti-depressants to children for acting like children, especially when they are actually suffering the effects of sugar-filled, unbalanced diets? Unless we as parents and health care practitioners step forward to take charge of our children's health, we will be mortgaging our future to the fast food, soda and pharmaceutical industries. The only return on our investment will be a generation of children that is poisoned and lethargic and who are candidates for addiction, chronic illness and pathological disease.

The LifeLine Technique successfully works for children who are too young to understand or actively participate in the treatment. I use a surrogate when a child is unable to consciously participate or is in a weakened state. Surrogate muscle testing involves the use of someone else's indicator muscle to assess another person who is unable to do it for him or herself. Surrogate muscle testing is based upon the principle that we are all electromagnetic beings. Thus, by touching another person anywhere on his or her body, you are able to connect to that individual through the use of your intent. The same is true of using a surrogate's arm to assess your own system. I often use my wife, Sara, as my surrogate to assess myself with The LifeLine Technique. Let me share with you several examples:

After seeing scores of doctors and undergoing every conceivable medical diagnostic test, including blood work, stool samples, urinalysis, allergy tests, etc., a mother brought her infant son to see me. Brian, who was less than a year old, suffered from severe allergies, skin rashes and eczema. The mother was breast feeding and I had her bring in foods she had been eating. Using her as a surrogate, I held those foods next to her body and next to Brian's body. Whenever I found a weak muscle, I harmonized his body to the food using The LifeLine Technique. As a result, I cleared the food allergies and released the internalized emotion that had triggered the allergic reaction. The mother was placed on Omega 3 Essential Fatty Acid and Probiotics, which she passed on to Brian. Within a month, Brian was 95 percent improved. After the mother's long odyssey seeking relief from doctor after doctor, she found it with The LifeLine Technique. Brian is now seen only for maintenance check-ups to help maintain his optimal health.

In another case, I received an emergency call on my day off from a patient whose five-year-old son, Jared, was confined to bed, unable to move his neck. Any attempt to move Jared resulted in severe pain and crying. His mother had to put "pull-up" diapers on him because the excruciating pain made a trip to the bathroom extremely difficult.

When I arrived at their home, I realized that Jared was experiencing a severe case of acute torticollis, which is a spasm of the sterno-cleido mastoid muscle located in the neck. I began by running the Conscious Body Portal of The LifeLine Technique, using Jared's mother as a surrogate. By touching his neck, the mother's arm went weak, allowing me to access the subconscious patterns that were creating this very painful symptom. After running The LifeLine Flow Chart through twice, Jared was able to get out of the bed and move his neck.

As we continued to work, the emotion of resentment came up. I soon discovered that Jared developed the symptoms on his baby brother's first birthday. We used the Conscious Mind Portal of The LifeLine Technique to tap into the internalized stress that was eating away at him, resulting in torticollis. By the time I finished, Jared was feeling much better. I advised his mother to use Arnica gel (a homeopathic) to assist with the relaxation of the muscles in his neck. I also communicated to both of them how important it was to drink water and own their power.

I reinforced with the mother how sensitive her son was and how important it was for her to express her unconditional love to him. To Jared, I said: "You're so lucky to be a big brother and to be able to celebrate this great day with your baby brother." He obviously had no conscious connection between the resentment over the celebration and the neck pain. However, by creating the awareness for Jared and his mother, the emotion was released on a subconscious level, allowing his body to heal instantly.

Symptoms are like the cover of a book. If you are walking around a bookstore, it is usually the cover that catches your eye; it intrigues you. You are drawn to open it, to look at its chapters in order to learn what the book is all about. Do not judge a book by its cover. This is how The LifeLine works. It reveals the "story" of the symptom to help you appreciate why your body is expressing itself. By exploring the symptom with The LifeLine Technique, you will learn from the "story"—which sometimes has many chapters—why the symptom has occurred in the first place. The more you explore the book—the symptom—using The LifeLine, the quicker you will find the solution.

Take the case of Rebecca, an eleven-year-old girl who was experiencing severe pain and muscle spasm in both of her legs, making it very difficult for her to walk. Unable to determine what was wrong, Rebecca's pediatrician recommended that she take an over-the-counter, anti-inflammatory drug, which did nothing to relieve the symptoms. The true root of the symptom, however, was unknown until she came in for a LifeLine treatment.

As I worked on Rebecca, running the symptom through The LifeLine Flow Chart, it became apparent that a major blockage was occurring in her root chakra. That chakra has to do with feeling grounded and secure and is tied in with limiting beliefs associated with family. The emotion of grief came up multiple times while running The LifeLine Flow Chart. I discovered that both of her great grandparents had recently died, within a month of each other, and that a close family member also was very ill and in the hospital.

After about twenty minutes of running The LifeLine Flow Chart, the pain in Rebecca's body decreased by about 90 percent. I discussed with her and her mother the importance of healthy lifestyles, which included drinking two quarts of water daily, avoiding sugar and carbohydrates, getting rest and owning her power. I explained to Rebecca that it was okay for her to express her emotions of sadness or grief. I encouraged her to allow her tears to flow if she felt like crying.

The next day, when I called to check on her, Rebecca's mother reported that it was really a miracle; Rebecca was doing amazingly well. But it really was not a miracle. It was The LifeLine Technique that allowed me to help them understand the true meaning of the symptoms Rebecca was feeling in her legs. By harmonizing the internalized emotions associated with the grief of her great grandparents' deaths, her body healed itself.

Just like the title of the Crosby, Stills and Nash song, "Teach Your Children Well" to value their health. I believe the first step is to educate parents to understand the importance of The Five Basics for Optimal Health and how they prevent the patterns of dis-ease and pathology from developing. Even before you have a child, you can optimize *your* health. As a matter of fact, I have helped scores of couples, who had been medically diagnosed infertile, become pregnant and deliver healthy babies by having them follow The LifeLine program.

At the same time, I want to make sure that parents are aware of the resources, alternatives and options available to help their children evolve and develop into happy, healthy and fulfilled human beings. Optimal health is a lifelong practice, but it begins with the first step: parents, both mothers and fathers, owning their power and taking responsibility for their children's health.

The LifeLine Technique in no way replaces the need for a pediatrician. However, in today's day and age, it is important that parents are empowered with information about the true nature of symptoms. By understanding The LifeLine Technique and philosophy, parents will be doing everything possible to provide safe, effective and natural ways to help maintain the optimal health of their children.

Parents have a choice about how to approach their children's health. One choice is to use medications to deal with the symptoms their children are facing. The other is to understand the natural expression of symptoms that the body uses to communicate. The latter, proactive choice will empower parents and children alike to heal in an authentic way.

Parents have the ultimate responsibility to protect their children's health by giving them love, embracing healthy lifestyles, creating appropriate boundaries and teaching them to own their power. The time to act for children is now!

CHAPTER THIRTY-ONE

Mastering the Game of Life

Life is so complex and chaotic at times, and yet there seems to be a sense of order and simplicity to the randomness. Depending upon your chosen view, you either align yourself with the order and simplicity or get lost and disconnect from the complexity and chaos. But what if life were a game? How would you play? What would the rules be? Most importantly, how would you master the game of life?

Let's begin with the rules.

1. THE UNIVERSE IS INFINITE.

Plato was speaking of the first rule of life when he said, "Mathematical objects, such as infinity, are real in their own right, and the mind has the power to grasp them directly in some way." From the concept of time and the cosmos, to the cycle of the seasons and life itself, the universe is infinite. It is forever expanding and undefined. Therefore, as a being of the universe, your mind possesses the nature and potential of the infinite. The infinite universe and mind are the great frontier, the endless entity of boundless mystery. Acknowledging your connection to the infinite universe and the infinite mind is fundamental to understanding the unlimited potential that you possess. This view is magnified to infinity by the core truth that you are a spiritual being having a human being experience. By be-ing, you experience the infinite essence and wonder of life.

2. YOU HAVE FREE WILL, A CHOICE WITH EVERY EXPERIENCE.

"To be or not to be, that is the question." Shakespeare taught the second rule of life when he wrote the play *Hamlet*. The act of "being" is a choice, a choice to stay connected to the moment, no matter how difficult it may be. Staying connected to the moment is living in Present Time Consciousness. When living in PTC, you awaken to the stream of consciousness and flow of thoughts that are always present within your mind. In PTC, your feelings are heightened and you tune into the subtleties of comfort and discomfort. You have a choice to stay in the comfort or discomfort or to disconnect from it. You have a choice "to be or not to be." Living in PTC enables you to trust your intuition and use your internal guides to help you flow from moment to moment. Even when it appears that you do not have a choice, you always do. Every moment is a mini-lifetime, a ripple in the ocean that manifests as the experience itself.

3. EVERYTHING IS INTERCONNECTED. FOR EVERY CHOICE THAT YOU MAKE THERE WILL BE A CONSEQUENCE.

Everything is interconnected in the infinite universe of energy. The LifeLine Law of Transformation and Creation states, "Emotions transform energy; energy creates movement; movement is change; and change is the essence of life." As a result of change, you experience life. From the fast or slow beat of a heart to the shallowness or depth of a breath, life moves forward through the action of duality, transformation and creation. It is by taking responsibility for your choices that you experience the flow of life and the greatest opportunities for growth. The consequences of your choices occur internally, within the body, as well as externally, in the universe of which you are a part. Every thought, feeling and belief either motivates you to choose to act out of fear or faith. This is the question that you should ask yourself before making a choice: "Am I making this choice out of fear or out of faith?" To be a master in the game of life, always choose faith. Be courageous and embrace the fear. Remember, movement and change are the essence of life and are the consequences of the choices that you make. Because 98 percent of your reality is subconscious, you may not always be aware of the consequences of your choices. However, for every choice that you make there will always be a consequence.

4. Judgment is prohibited.

Judgment is the lack of Present Time Consciousness. It is a reaction based upon preconceived notions about a person, race, religion, gender, nationality, etc. Living in PTC—embracing your intuition, feelings and beliefs—facilitates your ability to transcend judgment and make the best choices. Judgment is prohibited if you want to master the game of life. No matter what choices you have made in the past or what consequences you are now experiencing, stay in the moment and rediscover the lessons that your life has been teaching you. Remember, life is not about suffering and victimization. Life is about learning from your past and present so that you can experience your full potential. Every moment provides you with the opportunity to be in touch with your emotions and to react authentically. Do your best not to deny your intuition or feelings about an experience. Stay connected and trust your senses. You will then break the bonds of judgment.

5. The greatest power is self-love.

Unconditional acceptance, forgiveness and letting go are essential to unleashing the infinite power of self-love. Self-love acknowledges that the universe is perfect, and therefore you are perfect. Accepting your perfection is fundamental to unleashing your infinite potential, empowering you with the courage and determination to face the pain, fear and challenges of life. Self-love is the process of self-discovery—acknowledging, honoring and releasing the parts of yourself that you have subconsciously internalized, denied and disconnected from. The greatest adversary to self-love is fear. Resisting change because you fear losing your identity keeps the fear alive. Ralph Waldo Emerson once stated, "Self-trust is the essence of heroism." When you accept and own your power of self-love in a non-judgmental way, you embrace the fear that has kept you stuck in a cycle of self-denial and self-destruction. Self-love is the fuel—the passion—that motivates faith-based decisions. Being courageous in and of itself is an act of self-love.

6. You will experience pain, fear and challenges.

Throughout history, the greatest accomplishments have been achieved through determination, persistence, blood, sweat and tears. Everyone experiences pain, fear and challenges. It is the choices you make when faced with difficult situations that empower you to transform the experience into an opportunity for growth. Embracing this rule is vital to living a life without judgment. When you think about it, life would lack its quintessential beauty and meaning without pain, fear and challenges. By learning to face life with courage and passion, you appreciate the power you have always possessed to overcome life's greatest obstacles. These obstacles function innately as a self-defense mechanism to protect you from harm. By awakening to their inherent function, you continue to move, adapt and transcend life's most difficult experiences and transform them into triumph, abundance and peace. Embracing your power awakens you to the lessons and gifts that these challenges bestow. Learning the lesson and accepting the gift provides you with awareness, insight and power that you would have never achieved without the experience.

7. EMBRACE LIFE WITH THE ATTITUDE OF GRATITUDE.

The attitude that you have towards any experience is a choice. You can always view the cup as being half full or half empty. But the most courageous way to move through life is by choosing to find the good in every instance. Rather than surrendering to emotions of negativity and despair, consciously and creatively embrace life with the attitude of gratitude. Accepting challenges as opportunities immediately transforms the situation into an opportunity for developing your higher self. The act of expressing appreciation, such as saying "thank you," symbolizes the value an experience has had upon you. Without appreciation, life's experiences lack meaning, and your trials and tribulations appear as if they have occurred by coincidence. However, nothing in life is accidental. The attitude of gratitude expands your view of an experience beyond the "self" to an infinite perspective of possibilities and potential, thereby breaking the bond of suffering and victimization. By embracing pain, fear and challenges with gratitude, you will discover the real value and meaning of your life.

8. TAKE RESPONSIBILITY FOR YOUR LIFE.

As you have learned from reading this book, symptoms or challenges are your life's way of telling you to take responsibility. Think of living your life as the process of painting a masterpiece. Every breath, experience and intention adds to the beauty of your blank canvas. The vibrancy of the colors of life are felt when you love your-self unconditionally. It is with self-love that you are able to embrace the pain, fear and challenges of life and the infinite potential you have to transcend the most monu-mental of obstacles. Taking responsibility means you will make the choice to main-tain Present Time Consciousness despite the circumstances. It signifies that you will not judge the consequences of your choices, but rather learn from them. By choosing to take responsibility for your life, you will be inclined to embrace your experiences with the attitude of gratitude. Through gratitude you will find fortune in misfortune and step by step reconnect to the infinite potential of life. You are Michelangelo and the uncarved block awaits you. Create your "David." Each moment is an opportunity to release the artist within.

9. LIFE HAS MEANING.

Turn on the news and you will hear about war, genocide, political upheaval and scandals, poverty, starvation, racism, pollution, suicide, bankruptcy, death, hatred, violence, serial rapists, cancer, HIV-AIDS, children shooting each other, catastrophic floods and other natural disasters, gang violence, biological warfare, pedophiles, ter-rorism, financial coups, rampant obesity, domestic violence, spiraling divorce rates, resistant bacteria, increase in numbers of high school dropouts, infertility, decline in literacy, depression, road rage, drug overdose, carjackings, train bombings, assassi-nations, child molestation, pornography, addiction, ADD, celebrity court trials and tribulations, homophobia, sexism, conflicting values between generations, techno-logical breakdowns, nuclear weapons, international standoffs, overmedicating, rise in hospital death rates, malpractice, fear . . . fear . . . fear . . . fear . . . .

Can you imagine if life did not have meaning and all of these crises were occur-ring just because? This is our wake up call! Life is painful and yet there is meaning in pain. Life is scary and yet there is meaning in fear. Life is challenging and yet every challenge is an opportunity. We must ask the question why and be willing to hear the answer. We must own our power by embracing the infinite truth of a moment with-out judgement and with compassion and love. It is so easy to judge these experi-ences; however, we risk our future if we miss the opportunity to learn from our past and present.

Take a deep breath and reflect on the awesomeness of life. Have you ever seen the northern lights, a coral reef, or a baby being born? There is a rhythm and harmony that is an intricate part of every life process. Through science, humankind has revealed and unleashed some of the greatest mysteries of the universe. However, as much as science has taught us, it appears as if we are light years away from living at one with the universe. It is through meaning that we discover the preciousness of life—our own, as well as the lives of others. In the midst of horrific news and other life challenges, we often internalize, deny or disconnect from life's meaning. We succumb to illness, cynicism and hopelessness. But we have a choice—a choice to own our power, embrace life with passion and reconnect to the power of Infinite Love & Gratitude.

One single moment truly lived is the same as living a thousand lifetimes. The wisdom of the universe teaches us that each moment is truly experienced when we awaken to the power of Infinite Love & Gratitude, the key to mastering the game of life.

CHAPTER THIRTY-TWO

Imagine Yourself Healed

There is a Power whose magnificence is everywhere. We see this Power in every moment—in the sun, the rain and children playing. We hear it all around us—from the depths of silence to the crescendo of a symphony. The scent of that Power transforms our very souls—from a fragrant field of flowers to the freshness of a newborn baby. Every experience with this Power brings us closer to our authentic selves, to the source of God, the Divine or the collective conscious that is within all of us. It is the essence of every moment; it is Infinite Love & Gratitude.

We are always aware of this Power, even though we have numbed ourselves with food, alcohol, drugs, sex, work or relationships to make it easier to deny. In our denial, we are fearful, lonely, angry and judgmental. In our denial, we are bogged down in a dead-end, painful journey.

Allowing yourself to fully experience everything you see, hear, smell, touch, taste and create while subsequently acknowledging and accepting every resulting emotion, is an opportunity to own *your* power.

I implore you to begin your healing journey now. Reading this book has given you the tools—guidelines for healthy lifestyles coupled with a revolutionary healing technique that harmonizes the greatest adversary, your subconscious mind. Take the first step! Break out of your comfort zone. Let go of the belief that the state of your health—discomfort, dis-ease and dysfunction—is just "the nature of life." Let go of the guilty belief that chronic illness is the price you must pay for sowing "wild oats" when you were younger. Release the thought, feeling or belief that health is reserved only for the young, that aches and pains are a sign that you are "getting old." Popping pills, receiving injections or submitting to unnecessary surgeries are only temporary stopgaps. You may poke your fingers in a dam that has sprung multiple leaks, but eventually there will be an overflow, and the health you were fighting so hard to preserve will be lost.

Because your body is a self-healing organism, those aches, pains and chronic illnesses are actually a gift—a sign that you can *have* vibrant health if you are willing to claim it and do the work. Living in Present Time Consciousness, owning your power, embracing life with passion, and following healthy lifestyles that support harmony and balance in the body will help your body release the imbalances that lead to dysfunction and dis-ease.

Is it challenging? Yes! The years of internalization, denial or disconnecting from your emotions have molded a pattern that is easier to maintain than to change. However, you can break that pattern and use your newly acquired knowledge to enhance the quality of your own life. It starts with making a choice—a choice to imagine yourself healed.

Everything is possible! Your current state of health, your heredity, genetic predisposition, ethnicity or medical history *does not matter*! The LifeLine Technique is the bridge over troubled waters, the path from the world of dysfunction and disease to the world of freedom and passion. The choice is yours—the journey toward optimal health is simple. It begins with Infinite Love & Gratitude.

Rest assured, there will be internal doubts, obstacles and detractors lurking about. Change may not occur as fast as you want. There will be allopathic doctors who challenge you by saying, "You're incurable. You'll have irritable bowel syndrome, acid reflux, fibromyalgia, diabetes and hypertension, etc., the rest of your life." The process of change, however, requires determination and constant practice. Every symptom is an opportunity for healing. Every feeling of discomfort opens the door to health, growth and power. Every limiting belief, feeling or thought is a wall ready to be scaled.

Thomas Edison, the great American innovator, inventor and creative thinker, once said, "Many of life's failures are people who did not realize how close they were to success when they gave up." There is no failure in life when you do your best. There is no failure when you own your power, just the opportunity to learn lessons that will keep you on a course to achieve your highest goals—optimal health, dignity, happiness and peace of mind.

As Marianne Williamson has written in her book, *Return to Love: Reflections on the Principles of a Course in Miracles*: "We were born to make manifest the glory of God that is within us. It's not just in some of us, it's in everyone. When you liberate yourself from your own fears, your presence will automatically liberate others."

The process of healing is a spiritual journey, the evolutionary journey to awakening your spirit. Make it fun! Just remember, at the moment you choose to own your power and to *feel*, you have already succeeded.

Acknowledgements

There are many people who deserve thanks for the advent of this book. For those whom I have forgotten to mention, Infinite Love & Gratitude to you!

My friend and teacher, Jeri Love; your guidance through this incredible journey of writing has been invaluable. I am in awe of your wisdom, organization, and dedication. You are my rock, and I am infinitely grateful to you for helping me transform my inspiration and thoughts into a book. I could not have done this without you. Thank you for going the extra mile. Thank you! Thank you! Thank you!

Next, thanks to Dr. Thomas Bayne. Your foresight, big ideas and unending passion have motivated me to be my best.

I thank Dr. Ingrid Maes for challenging me to go beyond my limits, helping me to see that there are no limits. I am no longer afraid, and I have you to thank for that!

Thanks to Bob Sandidge and Anne Ward of CreativeCore. I do not know what Tom and I would have done without you. Everything is perfect, and it was part of the big plan that our paths have crossed.

Thank you, Jeffrey Sofferman and David Schiffman, for the greatest friendships a person could ever envision. I am blessed to have you both in my life. Thank you for your support, guidance and unconditional love. You guys are the best!

Thank you, Gina Stepuncik, for making The Way to Optimal Health a beautiful place for people to heal.

Thank you, Harlene Newman, for always saying the right thing at the right moment. You have an incredible skill for transforming lemons into lemonade.

Thank you to the thousands of people who have entrusted me with your health. I am infinitely grateful for the opportunity to be a part of your healing journey. You have helped me to heal, and I have grown so much as a result of our encounters.

A special thanks to Dee Michell, for showing me unending courage, love, and dignity throughout your life. Your journey has impacted me in a way that I am unable to purely express. You will always be in my heart.

Brian Goedhart, thank you for teaching me how to flow effortlessly and to live without judgement. You are the wizard of the *wind*.

Thank you, Dr. Roy Gonik, my beautiful friend. My life is so much richer with you in it. You are a gifted teacher and I treasure your friendship.

Thank you, Dr. Keith Jordan. You are so special to me. Luddy was a good boy.

Thank you, Kimball Paul, for your wisdom, grace and sharing your infinite knowledge of *The Way*.

Thank you, Ruth Bender, my friend and editor. Your skills of editing are only exceeded by your heart and authentic way you live your life.

To my Mom and Dad, I am so blessed to have chosen you. Thank you for giving me life. Your compassion, kindness and authentic way of living have molded me into the person I am today. I am so proud to be your son and to spread the Infinite Love & Gratitude with which you nurtured me to embrace within myself.

Thank you, Kenny, Paula, Rachel, Marc and Yoni Weissman, for your unyielding support and love. A special thanks to you, Paula, for your incredible editing skills and wonderful feedback. It was so helpful, and this book would not have been as beautiful without your insight and special touch.

Thank you, Howie, Nicole, Alex and Jacob Weissman. Howie, you have been a great teacher and friend. I have learned so much about myself, and I am forever grateful. I love you.

Thank you to all of my aunts, uncles, cousins and especially my Great Aunt Ethel. You are all so wonderful, and I feel so privileged to be a part of such an amazing family. What makes our family amazing is that we hold family traditions and connection as a top priority. It is something that has been handed down through generations, and I am thankful to be connected to such a rooted and extended family tree. I love you all very much!

Thank you, Martini/Anderson family for being the bonus to life. I feel so fortunate to be a part of your loving family.

Thank you, Floyd, Zen and Buddha (our cats), for your unconditional support and love. Your Taoist ways have awakened me to the subtle nature and joy of life. *Meow!*

I humbly express my Infinite Love & Gratitude to my daughter, Joya Ruth. Your mom and I are so blessed that you have chosen us as parents. I have a whole new appreciation for love with you in my life. You have helped me to recognize that every moment is a miracle waiting to happen.

Thank you, Sara, my beautiful wife, friend and lover. You are living proof that Infinite Love & Gratitude are what it is all about. Thank you for sharing life's journey with me. I look forward to the many adventures we will share. Thank you for your encouragement, for loving me for who I am, and for supporting me to own my power. With your tender and compassionate love, I am able to reach for the stars. I love you infinitely with all of my heart!

The LifeLine Technique
Glossary of Terms

Assemblage Point: The continuum of energy orbiting the midline of the body, moving along the microcosmic orbit, that represents the specific point in our superconscious where the internalization, denial or disconnection from our emotions originally occurred. The energetic disconnection within the subconscious mind.

Biochemical Expression: There are two forms of biochemical expression: meridian drainage (detoxifying the meridian by opening the routes of elimination and discharging the toxic accumulations) and meridian feeding (refers to hypo-function or less than optimal function of a corresponding meridian and the need for these areas to be fed with life force).

Body: The body is a mirror reflection of the energy that feeds its potential. Every thought, action and reaction is a reflection of the patterns that have programmed our bodies; programming begins the moment the sperm meets the egg.

Chakras: A Sanskrit word, "chakra" means *wheel* or *disk*. Chakras are the energy centers of the body. Each chakra moves with a spinning motion, forming a vortex. It is these vortices that filter the energy of the environment around us and disperse it through the seven chakras of the body. Chakras connect the body to the collective consciousness. They are the active component of the subconscious mind.

Chi: In Chinese medicine, *chi* refers to life force or electromagnetic energy. Chi is emotion.

Circadian Flow: The rhythmic flow of life force. In the Five Element Theory it refers to the two-hour period during the twenty-four-hour daily cycle in which each acupuncture meridian functions at its highest peak.

Collective Conscious: If there is a question, the answer can be awakened by channeling the collective conscious. The collective conscious is Infinite Love & Gratitude. Other names are the universe, macrocosm, the Divine, innate or God.

Conscious: The conscious is what our senses perceive and bring to the awareness of our higher mind. Two percent of our reality is conscious. The conscious part of the human brain is the cortex. Not until something becomes conscious can we learn or change.

Conscious Body Portal: Represents the subconscious patterns that are creating physical pain or inhibiting physical pain from healing. The Conscious Body Portal uses physical pain as a way into the subconscious mind, e.g., low back pain, headaches or stomach pain.

Conscious Mind Portal: Represents the subconscious patterns that are creating stressful situations in life or inhibiting you from releasing the stress. The Conscious Mind Portal provides awareness of the emotional connection to physical symptoms or stressful experiences in life, e.g., addictions, phobias, traumatic memories, panic attacks, etc. It can be used to set goals through declarative statements about where you are presently in life or where you would like to be.

Disease: A state of the physical body where there has been a pathological breakdown of at least 40 percent. When these pathological processes can be observed through diagnostics, such as blood tests, urine tests and radiographic procedures, a diagnosis can be given to that process. The medical profession treats disease. LifeLine Practitions treat people.

Dis-ease: *Dis-ease* = without ease. Physical discomfort as a result of stress, poor eating habits, the lack of water, exercise, rest and the internalization or denial of our emotions. It is the body's way of expressing imbalance.

Emotions: Any specific feeling; any of various complex reactions with both mental and physical manifestations, as love, hate, fear, anger, etc. Emotions can be broken down into two parts: "E" stands for energy, and "motion" implies movement, meaning *all emotions must stay in motion.* The subconscious internalization, denial or disconnection from emotions results in the manifestation of symptoms in the physical body. To achieve balance within the mind and body, one must authentically express his or her emotions.

Expression Channel: The Expression Channel enables the LifeLine Practitioner to know why an acupuncture meridian has a decreased flow in life force. It will always be either emotional, structural or biochemical.

The Five Basics for Optimal Health: The quantity, quality and frequency of water, food, rest, exercise and owning your power are the five components necessary for an optimally healthy lifestyle.

The Five Elements Theory: The Five Elements—Fire, Earth, Metal, Water and Wood—explain precisely where there is a decrease of life force in the body and in what way it is not flowing. The Five Elements help us to understand that the natural flow of energy which occurs within nature also occurs within the body.

Free Will: Free will is choice. No matter if we do not think, feel or believe we have a choice, we always do.

Frequency: A measure of electricity distinguished by the units of hertz. The body is electrical. Multiple frequencies make up and create the body. The vibrational frequency of the mind will determine the vibration in which the body will function. Low vibrations have a higher attractor field to imbalance and disease. High vibrational frequencies enable the body to release the holding patterns of imbalance, empowering the body to heal. Infinite Love and Gratitude has the highest of frequencies.

Frequency of Disease: A low vibrational frequency of the mind leads to stagnation within the body. Stagnation results in an accumulation of toxicity within the body, which will eventually lead to disease.

Harmonize: The restoration of balance between the mind, body and spirit occurs with the healing frequency of "Infinite Love & Gratitude."

Holding Pattern: It is the area in which a symptom is being held: the Mind, Body or Spirit. The holding pattern enables The LifeLine Practitioner to know where and why a symptom is being held in the body. The holding pattern represents subconscious addictions.

Holographic Principle: One part contains the whole of life, i.e., a single cell represents an entire being. When there is a symptom in one area of the body, the rest of the body also is holding the symptom. The LifeLine Technique focuses on a single symptom, emotional or physical, therefore balancing the entire person.

Ko: Each of The Five Elements has a relationship to the others. The Ko cycle is the destructive, or controlling, cycle.

The LifeLine Law of Transformation and Creation: Emotions transform energy; energy creates movement; movement is change; and change is the essence of life.

The LifeLine Technique: The LifeLine Technique is an evolutionary way to release the root cause of symptoms and disease. It uses muscle testing, a Flow Chart, and the healing frequency of "Infinite Love & Gratitude" to harmonize the subconscious internalized, denied or disconnected emotions that have resulted in symptoms. It is a fast, safe and powerful tool to release the root cause of symptoms. The cornerstone of The LifeLine Technique is The Five Basics for Optimal

Health—the quantity, quality and frequency of water, food, rest, exercise and owning your power. Anyone can be trained to use The LifeLine Technique.

Luo: The connection between the yin and yang acupuncture meridians of a particular element. The Luo cycle represents the interdependence of polar opposites.

Microcosmic Orbit: The microcosmic orbit is the circulating flow of energy that follows the Ren and Du acupuncture meridians along the midline of the body. This flow of energy has polarity and attracts and repels life experiences according to what we have subconsciously internalized, denied or disconnected from. The chakras are individual channels along the microcosmic orbit that connect the macrocosm of the collective conscious to the microcosm of the body. The microcosmic orbit is the mind.

Mind: The mind is composed of four parts: the conscious, subconscious, superconscious and collective conscious. The mind is the storehouse of our beliefs, which filter our perception of the environment and affect the autonomic function of the nervous system, triggering the sympathetic fright/flight/fight survival mode or parasympathetic relaxation/healing mode. The energy of Infinite Love & Gratitude connects the subconscious to the collective conscious.

Passion: Intense emotional drive or excitement, as in passion for life. Passion is the fuel for the will and is what gives life meaning.

Pathology: Pathology is diagnosable disease. For pathology to be present, the body needs to be broken down 40-plus percent.

Power Center: The Power Center is the area of The LifeLine Flow Chart that represents the subconscious mind. Also known as the superconscious or microcosmic orbit, the Power Center consists of the Mind (beliefs), Heart (feelings) and Will (thoughts). When we subconsciously internalize, deny or disconnect from our emotions, we are denying our power.

Present Time Consciousness (PTC): PTC is the act of staying connected to a moment, no matter how challenging, painful or scary. PTC enables you to acknowledge, honor and embrace your feelings; stay in tune with your senses and intuition; and live life without judgement. By authentically responding to what you are experiencing, PTC empowers you to live life with courage and faith, rather than out of fear.

Shen: Each of The Five Elements has a relationship to the others. The Shen cycle is the creative cycle.

Spirit: Spirit is the body's electromagnetic field or life force. Spirit is also known as *chi* or *prana*.

Subconscious: The subconscious mind is 98 percent of our reality. Pain, fear and challenges are the language used to communicate that we have subconsciously internalized, denied or disconnected from an emotion. It is through pain, fear and challenges that we discover the subconscious mind. The subconscious aspects of the brain are located in the limbic and reptilian centers.

Superconscious: The Superconscious is also known as the Power Center—Mind (beliefs), Heart (feelings) and Will (thoughts)—which connects us through the chakras to the collective conscious externally, as well as to the conscious and subconscious internally. The superconscious is the microcosmic orbit.

Symptoms: The language the body uses to communicate imbalance. Whether a symptom is physical or emotional, it is an opportunity the body gives us to heal on a deeper level. Symptoms are gifts that, when unwrapped, lead to the most extraordinary truths of our lives. Symptoms are the body speaking the mind.

Triad of Health: The Triad of Health represents the body in The LifeLine Flow Chart. The body can be separated into four parts—emotional, biochemical, structural and spiritual. It represents the specific location where an imbalance has occurred, leading to a decrease flow of life force.

Vibration/vibrational frequency: Vibrations are rapid back and forth, oscillating movements. Movement is change, and change is the essence of life. High vibrational frequencies naturally repel low vibrational frequencies. The LifeLine Technique removes roadblocks in the mind, body and spirit by harmonizing low vibrational frequencies with the healing frequency of Infinite Love & Gratitude.

Yang: The Chinese name given to represent positive, hollow, white, sky, external, male, active, above, kinetic or fire. Depending upon the perspective, something may be yang or yin. The yang acupuncture meridians are the outer meridians along the Five Elements.

Yin: The Chinese name given to represent negative, solid, black, earth, internal, female, passive, below, potential or water. Depending upon the perspective, something may be yin or yang. The yin acupuncture meridians are the inner meridians along the Five Elements.

Appendix A

Live Blood Cell Analysis

BEFORE: **AFTER:**

A 9 year-old boy with symptoms of severe migraine headaches.

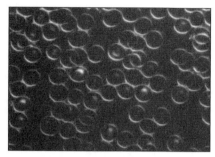

Using the power of Infinite Love & Gratitude, released subconscious feelings of internalized anger toward his parents because of their divorce.

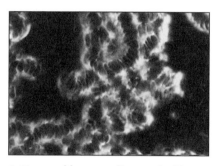

A 41 year-old woman diagnosed with breast cancer.

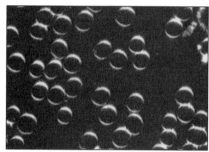

Using the power of Infinite Love & Gratitude, released subconscious feelings of depression associated with being emotionally and verbally abused by her husband.

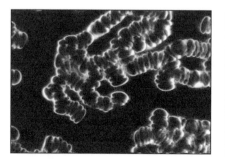

A 42 year-old man with symptoms of acid reflux.

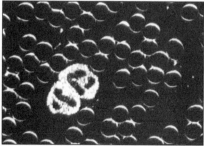

Using the power of Infinite Love & Gratitude, released subconscious thoughts of shame related to a family situation.

Before:

After:

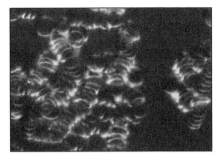

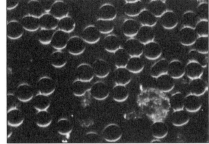

A 53 year-old woman with symptoms of insomnia.

Using the power of Infinite Love & Gratitude, released subconscious fears about her future because of the reorganization of the company where she worked.

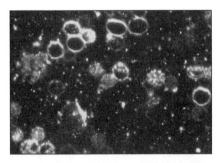

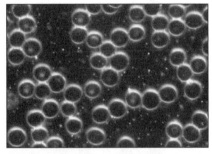

A 6 year-old boy with disruptive behavior; diagnosed with Attention Deficit Disorder (ADD).

Using the power of Infinite Love & Gratitude, released the subconscious feelings of frustration stemming from the birth of a sibling.

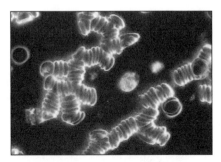

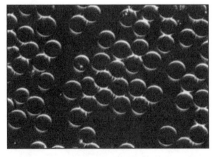

A 32 year-old woman diagnosed with fibromyalgia.

Using the power of Infinite Love & Gratitude, released subconscious feelings of grief she internalized for three years following the death of her mother.

BEFORE:

AFTER:

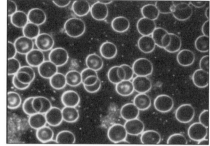

A 40 year-old woman whose attempts to get pregnant had been unsuccessful.

Using the power of Infinite Love & Gratitude, released the subconscious beliefs that her age made it impossible to get pregnant. She had a baby 11 months later.

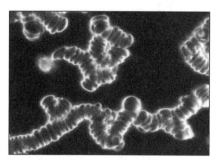

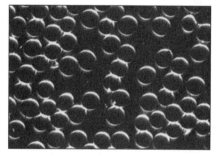

A 50 year-old woman plagued with environmental allergies.

Using the power of Infinite Love & Gratitude, released the subconscious thoughts and feelings of fear and shame stemming from childhood sexual abuse.

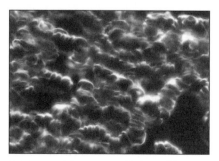

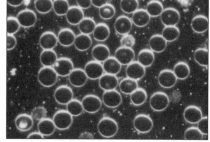

A 36 year-old woman suffering with severe neck pain.

Using the power of Infinite Love & Gratitude, released subconscious feelings of jealousy of a co-worker who received a promotion.

218

BEFORE:

AFTER:

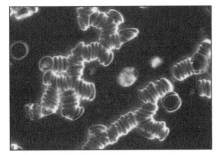

A 20 year-old college athlete with a pulled hamstring muscle.

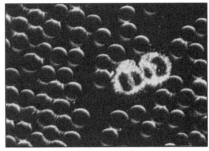

Using the power of Infinite Love & Gratitude, released subconscious feelings of grief related to the death of his grandmother.

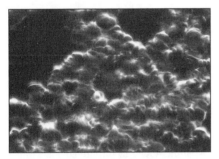

A 53 year-old woman with severe peri-menopause symptoms, including mood swings and hot flashes.

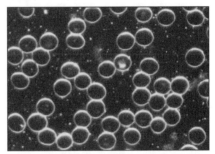

Using the power of Infinite Love & Gratitude, released subconscious fears arising from suddenly being responsible for her elderly father.

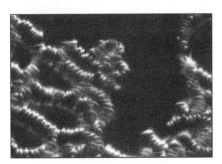

A 60 year-old man who suffered with panic attacks for 15 years.

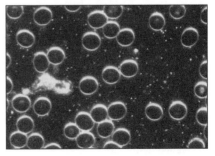

Using the power of Infinite Love & Gratitude, released subconscious feelings of contempt resulting from an argument he had with his boss that occurred the week before the advent of the attacks.

BEFORE:

AFTER:

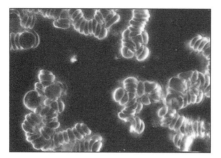

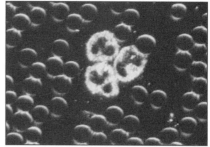

A 12 year-old child who suffered with severe fatigue.

Using the power of Infinite Love & Gratitude, released subconscious feelings of dread about going to middle school.

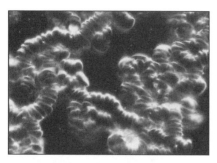

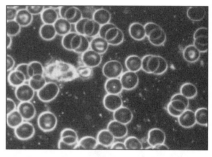

A 38 year-old woman who had severe symptoms of tingling and numbness but all of her medical tests were negative.

Using the power of Infinite Love & Gratitude, released subconscious thoughts of self-dislike stemming from her childhood.

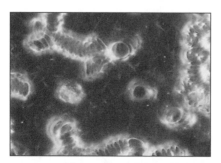

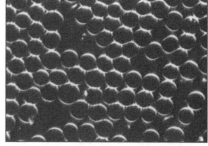

A 29 year-old man complaining of bursitis in his shoulder.

Using the power of Infinite Love & Gratitude, released subconscious feelings about being smothered by his mother.

BEFORE:

AFTER:

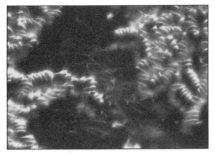

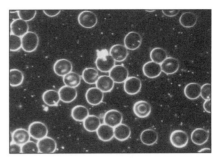

A 14 year-old with severe blood sugar metabolism imbalances.

Using the power of Infinite Love & Gratitude, released subconscious anger about being harassed by a bully at school.

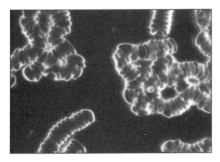

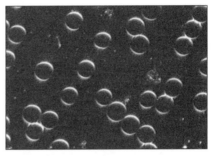

A 75 year-old, recent widow with severe dizziness.

Using the power of Infinite Love & Gratitude, released subconscious anxieties about her future.

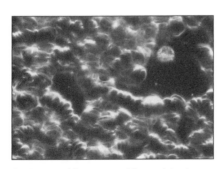

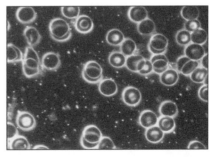

A 43 year-old woman with persistent upset stomach.

Using the power of Infinite Love & Gratitude, released subconscious beliefs that she should be perfect.

BEFORE:

AFTER:

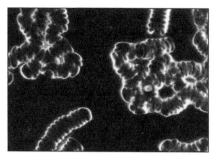

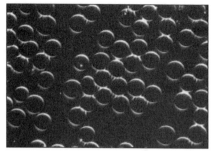

A 31 year-old man diagnosed with kidney stones.

Using the power of Infinite Love & Gratitude, released subconscious feelings of powerlessness in the wake of cutbacks and decreased job security at work.

Information and Resources

The LifeLine Technique

Dr. Darren Weissman

The Power of Infinite Love & Gratitude

The LifeLine Technique Seminars

Certification for LifeLine Practitioners

Wellness Products

www.infiniteloveandgratitude.com

(866) 398-9864

Total Body Modification

Dr. Victor Frank

www.tbmseminars.com

Neuro-Emotional Technique

Dr. Scott Walker

www.netmindbody.com

International College of Applied Kinesiology

Dr. George Goodheart

www.icak.com

Hidden Messages in Water

Dr. Masaru Emoto

www.hado.net

Biology of Belief

Dr. Bruce Lipton

www.brucelipton.com

Neuro-Linguistic Programming

Tim and Kris Halbom

Wealthy Mind Seminars

www.themoneyclinic.biz

www.nlpca.com

Dr. Joe Mercola

www.mercola.com

What the Bleep Do We Know?

www.whatthebleep.com

Recommended Reading

A Better Way to Live, by Og Mandino

Ageless Body, Timeless Mind, by Deepak Chopra, M.D.

Anatomy of the Spirit, by Caroline Myss, Ph.D.

A Return to Love: Reflections on the Principles of "A Course in Miracles," by Marianne Williamson

The Art of Happiness, His Holiness The Dalai Lama and Howard C. Cutler, M.D.

Body Electric: Electromagnetism and the Foundation of Life, by Robert Becker, M.D.

Chi Nei Tsang, by Mantak and Maneewan Chia

Conversation with God (Series 1-3), by Neale Donald Walsh

Cross Currents: The Promise of Electromedicine, the Perils of Electropollution, by Robert Becker, M.D.

DMT: The Spirit Molecule, by Rick Strassman, M.D.

Embracing Our Selves, by Hal Stone Ph.D. and Sidra L. Stone, Ph.D.

EMDR, by Francine Shapiro, Ph.D. and Margot Silk Forrest

The Four Agreements, by Don Miguel Ruiz

Getting the Love You Want, by Harville Hendrix, Ph.D., and Helen Hunt, Ph.D.

The Gift of Fear, by Gavin DeBecker

Infinite Mind: Science of the Human Vibrations of Consciousness, Valerie V. Hunt

Man's Search for Meaning, by Viktor Frankl

Many Lives, Many Masters, by Brian Weiss, M.D.

Mastery of Love, Don Miguel Ruiz

Molecules of Emotion, by Candace B. Pert, M.D.

The Power of Intention, by Dr. Wayne W. Dyer

Power vs. Force: The Hidden Determinants of Human Behavior, by David R. Hawkins, M.D.

Psycho-Cybernetics, by Maxwell Maltz, M.D., F.I.C.S.

The Seven Spiritual Laws of Success, by Deepak Chopra, M.D.

The Sugar Control Bible and Cookbook, by Dr. Jacqueline Paltis, D.C., N.D.

Traditional Acupuncture: The Law of the Five Elements, by Dr. Diane Connelly

There's a Hole in My Sidewalk, by Portia Nelson

There's a Spiritual Solution to Every Problem, by Wayne W. Dyer

The Story of Edgar Cayce: There Is a River, by Thomas Sugrue

The Tibetan Book of Living and Dying, by Sogyal Rinpoche

Twenty-five things every new mother should know, by Martha Sears, R.N., with William Sears, M.D.

The Way of Energy, by Master Lam Kam Chuen

Visioning: Ten Steps to Designing the Life of Your Dreams, Lucia Capacchione, Ph.D., A.T.R

Wheels of Life: A User's Guide to the Chakra System, by Anodea Judith

Why People Don't Heal and How They Can, by Caroline Myss, Ph.D.

Your Body's Many Cries for Water, by F. Batmanghelidj, M.D.

Your Body Speaks Your Mind, by Debbie Shapiro